VIETNAM REFLECTIONS

Vietnam Reflections: The Untold Story of the Holley Boys

ISBN: 978-0-9975641-0-5

Cover by MS Illustration and Design

Interior Design by Country Mouse Design
www.countrymousedesign.com

VIETNAM REFLECTIONS

THE UNTOLD STORY OF

The Holley Boys

Michael T. Keene

ALSO BY

MICHAEL T. KEENE

BOOKS

Folklore and Legends of Rochester
Murder, Mayhem & Madness
The Psychic Highway
Question of Sanity
Mad House
Abandoned

FILMS

The Murder of William Lyman
The Strange Disappearance of Captain William Morgan
In Search of White Crows
The Code of Handsome Lake
Visions

AUDIO BOOKS

Anthology

They are not dead who live in the hearts they leave behind.

—Tuscarora

IN MEMORIAM

David P. States

4/15/1945 10/17/1966

He was a great person and ready to help anyone

CONTENTS

Introduction 13
Chapter 1. Welcome to Holley 17
Chapter 2. Why Vietnam? 27
Chapter 3. John P. Davis 35
Chapter 4. Dien Bien Phu 43
Chapter 5. David D. Case 49
Chapter 6. Diem Assassination 61
Chapter 7. Ronnie P. Sisson 67
Chapter 8. Gulf of Tonkin 79
Chapter 9. Howard L. Bowen 83
Chapter 10. My Lai Massacre 93
Chapter 11. Gary E. Bullock 99
Chapter 12. Tet Offensive 113
Chapter 13. Garry L. Stymus 117
Chapter 14. Bombing of Cambodia 129
Chapter 15. George W. Fischer, Jr. 133
Chapter 16. The End Game 145
Chapter 17. Paul S. Mandracchia 153
Conclusion 169
Acknowledgements 175
Appendix 177
Notes 215
Bibliography 223
Index 227

INTRODUCTION

The Vietnam War was a long and costly armed conflict that pitted the Communist regime of North Vietnam and its southern allies, known as the Viet Cong, against South Vietnam and its principal ally the United States.

The war, for all intents and purposes began for the United States in 1954. Following the French defeat at Dien Bien Phu by Ho Chi Minh and his Communist Viet Minh Party in North Vietnam, the war continued for the next 20 years against the backdrop of an intense Cold War between the two global superpowers: the United States and the Soviet Union.

Beginning with the Geneva Accords that were established to ostensibly allow general elections between the north and south (that were never held), the United States became increasingly involved in Vietnam with the introduction of U.S. military advisors whose role was to assist the South Vietnamese government.

In 1963, the then President of South Vietnam, Ngo Dinh Diem, and his brother, Ngo Dinh Nhu, his chief advisor, were assassinated. It is generally accepted that their assassination was orchestrated at least in part, with the acquiescence of the administration of President John F. Kennedy. At the time of Kennedy's assassination just three weeks later, there were a total of 16,000 U.S. advisors in South Vietnam.

In one of history's more bizarre events, in an incident that may not have even happened, an attack in the Gulf of Tonkin on an American Navy ship by a North Vietnamese patrol boat, propelled the United States ever deeper into the Vietnamese conflict. This would set the stage for the Gulf of Tonkin Resolution, which upon passage by the Senate (by a vote of 88-2) allowed the president, Lyndon B. Johnson, to begin a massive bombing campaign against North Vietnamese targets.

American ground troops were introduced in earnest in early 1965. By the end of that year 165,000 U.S. combat forces were in Vietnam.

By 1969, at the war's zenith, more than 550,000 U.S. military personnel were involved in the conflict. Over 58,000 troops were killed, and 300,000 wounded by the war's end.

Protests against the Vietnam War became widespread. As the result of the bombing of Cambodia, a demonstration was held at Kent State University resulting in the shooting deaths of four students by the Ohio National Guard.

The U.S. government, under tremendous pressure to end its involvement in Vietnam, began to draw down the presence of combat troops. Re-elected in 1972 with the promise that 'peace was at hand', Richard M. Nixon ordered the total withdrawal of all U.S. forces in 1973.

During the course of America's involvement in the Vietnam War many American communities experienced terrible losses. None suffered more than the small rural farming town of Holley, New York.

Located thirty-five miles west of Rochester, New York, eight boys from the rural farming community of Holley died while serving in Vietnam. All of them went to the same high school where the average graduating class numbered just 30 students. The casualty rate was one of the highest of any town and school in America, rivaling even the carnage experienced by many Northern states during the Civil War. Collectively, the 'Holley boys' were awarded 40 medals for combat and valor including seven Purple Hearts, the Bronze Star, Silver Star and the Vietnamese Cross for Gallantry.

But they were more than soldiers and heroes. They played Little League, were Boy Scouts, went to sock-hops and performed in the high school marching band. They also drove hot-rods, drank beer, smoked, and brawled. They weren't angels. They were boys—once.

Now, nearly 50 years later, their stories are told. Drawing upon over 60 interviews with family members and friends, personal letters, diaries, after action combat reports, newspaper accounts of the day, and military archives, *Vietnam Reflections: The Untold Story of the Holley Boys* reveals to us not only the lives of these boys, but also a seldom seen look at American society during that period, and a remarkable small town you probably never heard of, before that damn war changed everything.

CHAPTER ONE

Welcome to Holley

"I am thinking of a village that pulses with life, whose curbs are lined with farmers' cars; whose high school resembles a baronial castle; whose fire hall is replete with shiny, modern apparatus; whose pride is boundless in its athletic teams, bands, volunteer fire department, veterans' posts and churches.

"Of course, I have in mind a particular community . . . This particular village has a distinctive public square, green with shrubs. The business places of the town flank it on four sides. At its head in a tall church tower the village clock ticks off the long years. The village's very name brings to mind bright red berries, green leaves and Christmas time although they have naught to do with its name. I've kept you in suspense too long. Ladies and gentlemen, I give you Holley, N. Y."

~ *The Towpath* by Arch Merrill

THE VILLAGE OF HOLLEY IS A SMALL DOT ON THE MAP. But, of course, that depends on who's looking for it or who calls it home. Like many primal pieces of land, Holley, too, was once the domain of native wild animals who roamed through the thickly rooted underbrush of shrubs, plants and hearty hemlock trees. When Holley's first settlers arrived in 1802, many reported that the trees were so thick and wide that they could stand in the forest on a day of bright sunshine, and still be surrounded by total darkness.

A Clearing on the Horizon

Cheap, fertile land was available for sale, yet all of it was uncultivated wilderness. Settlers were encouraged when news surfaced about the construction of a grand canal from Albany to Buffalo.

Myron Holley (1779 -1841)—the man for whom the village would eventually be named—was instrumental in literally getting the project—and so many trees—off the ground.

Myron Holley, the town of Holley's namesake, who personally supervised a 158 mile swath of the Erie Canal that ran from the Seneca River to Buffalo.

Like other adventurous young men of his time, the Connecticut born and educated Holley decided to satisfy his curiosity about finding fortune on New York's rugged frontier and settled in Canandaigua, New York in the early 1800s. He opened a book store, then met and married Sally House, with whom he had six sons and six daughters.

He was also a lawyer and in 1810 his political career in the village began as county clerk. In 1816 he was named as the county's representative to the New York State Assembly and met DeWitt Clinton. Holley embraced Clinton's bold idea for the construction of the great canal and soon became an ardent advocate for the mammoth waterway that would forever change America in every economic, societal, humanistic and spiritual way.

In support of the idea, Holley wrote convincing reports to the legislature about the efficacy of newly invented machinery to aid in the canal's construction, like the massive tree stump puller; the three-wheel wheelbarrow and a winching device to extract ancient tree trunks and rocks.

His correspondence was positively acknowledged and Holley was appointed to the first Erie Canal Commission, serving with Joseph Ellicot, Samuel Young, Stephen Van Rensselear and DeWitt Clinton. Clinton was named as president; Young as secretary and Holley as treasurer.

Finding a "Salt-Lick"

In 1812, two of Holley's earliest pioneers were entrepreneurs William Rice and Stephen Lewis who also saw the financial potential of this unchartered place. They intended to establish a town—a *canal town*—right on the path of the proposed canal. In 1814, businessman John Reed made an important discovery: a "salt-lick". A salt-lick or mineral lick was a place wild animals frequented to "lick" essential nutrients from natural salt or mineral deposits.

Reed jumped at the prospect of creating a business from this discovery. He knew that salt was a necessity for the preservation of the settlers' food, but it needed boiling and processing. He went about accomplishing this and became the area's first manufacturer of salt. That's when the small village was dubbed "Saltport". (1)

~

Financier Aerovester Hamlin also envisioned the formation of a working village on the canal route. In 1822, he purchased 100 acres of land and had it surveyed and plotted, with streets radiating out from the central square.

Hamlin anticipated shops and dwellings on three sides of the village and docks and warehouses on the remaining east side. Up until the completion of the Erie Canal in 1825, there were just six buildings in the entire village. When the canal construction in Saltport was completed in 1823, Hamlin's dream became a reality. He then built his own mansion on the east side of the canal where he could view his holdings in the square and on the busy docks. He also created a village post office. In 1828, however, Hamlin's zealous overspending compelled him to sell his holdings. Hiram Frisbie and James Seymour purchased most of his property.

As construction of the canal soared, so too did the population of the village. Settlers and businesses prospered, largely through farming the rich soil for vegetable crops and fruit orchards. Shipping their abundant harvests via the Erie Canal was easily facilitated.

A Hands-on Effort

Myron Holley and Samuel Young personally supervised and paid the canal workers, continually traveling with them along the route, often through stubborn overgrowth and dense countryside. They travelled in open wagons, on horseback and even on foot over exceptionally treacherous terrain. At the end of a freezing cold or oppressively hot, grueling work day, Holley would dutifully hole up in a candle-lit makeshift shanty to summon and pay the workers.

Rochester Thanks You!

Holley was specifically in charge of the canal construction west of the Seneca River for approximately 158 miles to Buffalo. In a letter to Benjamin White, the chief engineer of the project, Holley made sure the path of the canal would go directly through Rochester:

" . . . proceed to Rochester and ascertain carefully where the Genesee should best be crossed . . . lay out the line easterly . . . divide into suitable section for actual contract. To these directions he industriously conformed," wrote Holley.

Bypassing Canandaigua and Batavia to the south was crucial to the building of the canal to ensure the continuous natural water supply of creeks and streams in those areas.

After the completion of the Erie Canal in 1825, Holley enjoyed a quiet private life with his grandchildren and pursued his interest in horticulture. He also enjoyed raising choice fruits and vegetables, such as pears and asparagus. He was known by friends and neighbors as kind and affable, yet outspoken about social causes. He was prominent in the anti-Masonic, Temperance and anti-Slavery movements.

The wife of a local doctor once remarked:

"I have seen a true gentleman! He came to the basement door selling vegetables!"

"Oh yes," replied her husband. *"That was Myron Holley."*

The Rochester Freeman

In 1837, Myron Holley bought a printing press and used it to produce the abolitionist newspaper, the *Rochester Freeman*, introducing anti-slavery sentiments to the people of Rochester and related Northern cities. It is said that the availability of the newspaper laid the foundation for the Underground Railroad in Rochester and its surrounding communities.

At a speaking engagement in Rochester in 1847, Frederick Douglass stated:

"The ground had been prepared for me by the labor of others, notably Hon. Myron Holley. I know of no place in the Union where I could have located with less resistance, or received a larger measure of sympathy and cooperation."

A Final Farewell to a Fine Man

From the time settlers first arrived in 1812, canal communities rose up and profited from the fertile farmlands of the Erie Canal corridor. That tradition continues today, to some extent.

At 8 a.m. on March 4, 1841, bells rang from Rochester's churches and City Hall commemorating the inauguration of President William Henry Harrison. Ironically, the day also marked the passing of Myron Holley.

Canal families honored him by suggesting to Rochester land surveyor, Elisha Johnson, that their canal-side village of Saltport be renamed for Myron Holley. The village was incorporated in 1850 and renamed Holley, New York. (2)

Early Settlers 1800-1830

Other notable personalities of the day, with strong, serious-sounding names—and some with lighthearted stories to report—settled in Holley and set the tone for the kind of neighbor-oriented, work-hard-do-good credo that defined the village and the virtuous "stock" its people imparted.

Hubbard Price moved to the town of Murray, which adjoined the village of Holley, in 1802 with his father's family. "He grew up to manhood there, seeing and sharing in all the toils, dangers, hardships and privations which settlers endured," notes Arad Thomas in "The Pioneer History of Orleans County, NY".

Abner Balcom, originally from Otsego County, New York, was brought up in Hopewell in Ontario County and moved to Murray in 1810. In 1813, he and his brother, Horace, cleared 22-acres of land on the lot Horace purchased in 1816. This was the first clearing of a substantial lot in Murray, located on the line between Ridge and Clarendon.

His son, Francis Balcom, volunteered for the Union Army in the first years of the Civil War, and was killed in battle, "gallantly fighting to save the country which the instructions of his father and instincts of his own nature had taught him to love."

Elijah W. Wood originally of Pelham, Massachusetts, moved to Murray "at an early day" and served as Constable and Justice of the Peace and for one term (five years) as a Judge in the Old Court of Common Pleas in Orleans County.

"He was a shrewd and successful pettifogger in justices' courts, where he made up in wit and natural sagacity any lack he may have suffered in legal attainments. He died in Murray at the age of eighty years."

Alanson Mansfield, arriving in town in 1814, must have resembled a true pioneer, toting an ax, which pretty much constituted his entire personal estate. He settled in and proceeded to "chop" in the town of Murray until he'd earned enough money to purchase a land lot north of Hindsburg. That's when he returned to his Vermont home, gathered his entire family—his father, his mother and six siblings ---into a sleigh, led by a pair of horses and a milk cow trailing behind. Their provisions consisted of a barrel of pork, some meat and some basic household goods.

In the winter of 1815, he built a log house for the family and cleared timber from the land. Their first seasonal crop was corn. He joined the Holley Baptist Church in 1831 and was a "worthy, honored man . . . respected by all who knew him."

Health conscious ancestors of **Chauncey Robinson** would appreciate his words: "I have never used one pound of tea, coffee, or tobacco, and comparatively little liquor; none for the last thirty years; not even cider. My constant drink at home and abroad is cold water."

Robinson was born in Durham, Connecticut in 1792. When he was two-years-old, his father carried him to Sauquoit, Oneida County, New York, accompanied by his entire family. "I was educated in a district school, and graduated, at twelve years of age, between the plow handles," Robinson said. It is recorded that in his personal habits, he was industrious, frugal and temperate.

Another brave soul, **Aretas Pierce**, was born in St. Johnsbury, Vermont, in 1799 and settled with his family in Clarendon in 1815. His story is rather short and uneventful compared to others of his time. The first year they arrived, the Pierce family lived on the provisions they brought with them. The next year, in the cold season, they bought rye at $1.25 a bushel and pork at $25 a barrel. The following year, the family ran out of "bread stuff" before harvest and "ate green wheat boiled in milk as a substitute . . . and what is strange none of the family had dyspepsia (indigestion)."

Austin Day came to Murray "some years" after his birth in Windhall, Vermont, in 1789. He was described as being "a good talker" who practiced *pettifogging* and served as Constable and/ or acted as Counsel in Justice Courts for several years, "until professional lawyers came in." He was said to "do a large business." He was elected Sheriff of Orleans County in 1847. He held the office for three years. In 1848, he moved to Albion and passed way in 1852.

Harley N. Bushnell was born in Starksborough, Vermont in 1796, the youngest of 13 children. He went to Connecticut when he was 15 years-old to learn the trade of clothier, then apprenticed for five years. In Holley, he served as Superintendent of the Presbyterian Sunday School. He was known as a kind-hearted, genial man; benevolent and philanthropic; "earnest and zealous" in every good cause and "died lamented by all who knew him."

Hiram Frisbie came to Orleans County from Granville, New York, with "a view" of taking a job. In 1821, with his brother-in-law, William Pierpont, he opened a store selling "pot and pearl ashes" or potash, which is a generic term for water soluble potassium salts that are mined or manufactured. Since its discovery, potash has been used in the manufacture of glass, ceramics, soap and fertilizer (as potassium oxide). Pierpont also sold a tavern he owned to Frisbie, who managed it alone for several years. When other merchants in Holley went out of business, Frisbie capitalized on their holdings by building houses, selling village lots and opened streets, all of which made him quite wealthy.

After **Reuben Bryant** was admitted to the bar of the Supreme Court, he settled his law practice in Holley in 1823, earning the title of "pioneer lawyer". He was born in Templeton, Worcester County, Massachusetts in 1792 and graduated from Brown University in Rhode Island in 1815. He did some teaching in Livingston County, and studied law under the late Judge Smith in Caledonia. It was recorded, "He was a thorough classical scholar, and had his mind well stored with Greek and Latin lore, which he delighted to quote in social moments with his friends when circumstances made it proper."

Jacob Hinds, of Arlington, Bennington County, Vermont, settled in the town of Murray in 1829. He bought a farm, then built a grocery store and began a business in a location good for growing and shipping wheat. In 1830, Hinds built a warehouse. His brothers, Joel, Darius and Franklin—"active, energetic businessmen"—joined the business. Soon, the area was called Hindsburgh.

Last, but not least, are the "recollections of **Mrs. Sally Smith**", who was born in 1795 in St. Johnsbury, Vermont and moved with her family to LeRoy, New York, in 1816. "We were twenty-one days on the journey," she wrote. By 1817, Mrs. Smith was teaching school in Murray's District No. 8, in a log house where a local family actually lived. "My wages were nine shillings a week and boarded among my patrons. I taught eight months during which time I was happy and fared well," she recorded. She married Artemas Daggett in 1819 and worked on their farm. "Mr. Daggett died in 1831 and left me with three small children and one hundred acres of land, owing about nine hundred dollars. In two years I raised the money and paid our debts and took a deed of the land. About this time, I married Isaac Smith, with whom I lived in peace and plenty until his death in August, 1866," wrote the industrious Mrs. Smith. (3)

"A Beautiful Place to Live and Visit"

Settlers bravely challenged their new, untamed environment with virtually no prior knowledge of the land, the weather, the cultures of others who may have come before them, or of starting businesses for survival and trade. Tenacity and hope led them to betterment and personal accomplishment. And, they maintained it, praying for health, the Lord's blessings and time to reap another harvest. Few became truly wealthy; but the average man made his mark, satisfied and proud at the end of the day.

Holley is often referred to as "a great place to call home". Many may feel that way about their own cities or towns. But, close-knit communities like Holley are strengthened by the empathy and shared experiences—good or bad—of its residents. When something happens to one neighbor, it happens to everyone.

By the 1960s Holley was like many small towns in America, somewhat isolated and immune to the whirl of international events. But that would all change in a place 10,000 miles away that would have profound repercussions and tragedy for the country and utter devastation for Holley. That place was Vietnam.

CHAPTER TWO

Why Vietnam?

EVERYONE HAD AN OPINION about the Vietnam War, before, during and after, right up to the present day. Many of those perspectives have never changed. Along with growing Civil Rights unrest, the Anti-War movement, sparked by America's participation in the war, was one of the most divisive forces in the history of the United States. The ongoing debate and the reactions it aroused touched all rungs of society—politically, racially, socially and culturally—creating a deep, tumultuous upheaval of sentiment across the country and the world.

What was it about this war that struck such discordant tones in America and beyond? A brief look back at the political history of this enigmatic, "S" shaped country in Southeast Asia—often described by the Vietnamese as a bamboo pole supporting a basket of rice on each end—may help to explain its turbulent past.

Location

Vietnam's coastline stretches for 2,144 miles and the nation shares 2,373 miles of borders with China, Laos and Cambodia and maritime borders with the Gulf of Thailand, the Gulf of Tonkin and the South China Sea. The country's northern land region is quite broad, narrowing in the middle and down through its southern reaches. At one point, the width of the country is just 31 miles.

The majority of the land is covered by rainforest and thick, heavy foliage; almost half of its terrain is mountainous. Two important river systems characterize Vietnam's topography, the Red River in the north and the Mekong River in the south. The Red River Delta in the north offers rich, grain producing conditions and, consequently, is more heavily populated than the Mekong Delta in the south. Rice, the country's most significant crop, is grown everywhere; today, the majority of it comes from the fertile Mekong Delta. (1)

Early Civilizations and Political Rule

> *"Vietnamese history is characterized by two themes. The first is the effort to preserve the national identity against foreigners. The second theme is territorial expansion, most notably the march to the south... Pham Quyunh noted the repeated divisions that wars have caused his country: 'We are a people in search of a country – and we do not find it.'"*
>
> ~ *Spencer Tucker, historian*

It is believed that Vietnam's earliest peoples migrated from the islands of Indonesia and settled on the shores of the Red River in the Tonkin Delta. A pre-historic kingdom of sorts emerged and took hold in the area between the Red and Mekong Rivers. This ancient civilization surfaced in the Paleolithic Era (a period of human history distinguished by the creation and implementation of stone tools). The population was a compilation of Malayo-Polynesian people (from Java, Malaysia, Thailand and Northern Burma) who had adopted aspects of Indian and Indonesian religious beliefs and methods of trade.

Vietnam's expansive coastline provided access and settlement of the country by many seafaring groups. By its medieval period, Vietnam resembled a "melting pot" of ethnicities, languages, social customs, and religious and cultural values. (2)

1,000 Years of Chinese Domination

In 111 BC northern Vietnam was ruled by China's Han Dynasty; a seminal condition that would initiate a long series of historical occupations and military invasions by subsequent Chinese and Mongol dynasties. The Chinese teachings of philosopher Confucius (551 - 479 BC) taught obedience and loyalty to the early peasant population of Vietnam, who were heavily taxed and unpaid for working on roads, temples and the buildings of landowners. This exploitation spurred frequent rebellions among the populace. Few resulted in Vietnamese independence. Chinese rule would consistently overturn and outweigh the uprisings, thus recapturing political control.

A compromised Vietnamese independence occurred in the 10th century when invading Chinese forces were defeated by Viet general Ngo Quyen. His successor, warlord Dinh Bo Linh, opted to rule Vietnam as a vassal state, agreeing that the Vietnamese would abide by Chinese law. For the next nine centuries northern Vietnam (called Dai Vet) was ruled by local dynasties. Southern Vietnam (called Champa) was less officially ruled or governed by a recognized government, but existed as an affiliation of tribal groups. The "Cham" people were less influenced by the Chinese than those in the north. Bordering powers to the west had greater influence on the people of southern Vietnam.

Throughout the 13th century, civil wars between factions in the north and south prevailed. In 1370 the Cham invaded the north, getting as far as the city of Hanoi. They were soundly defeated by what would emerge as Vietnam's longest ruling empire, the Le Dynasty. In 1470 Le armies destroyed the Champa kingdom, entirely. (3)

Under French Rule

From the late 1800s to 1954, Vietnam was part of a French colony called French Indochina. In 1859 the French captured Saigon and in 1883, north and central Vietnam became a French protectorate.

However, the French presence in Vietnam did not happen all at once, but was gradually accomplished, beginning as early as the 16th century when European missionaries arrived, intending to convert the native population to Catholicism. They also possessed technical skills and connections to European suppliers of weapons and Western merchandise. French merchants initially saw trade opportunities in the country's coffee, tea and rubber resources and envisioned a long-lasting presence in Southeast Asia. By 1688, the French East India Company had been formed and continued its existence for centuries. (4)

A History of Rebellion

The tradition of armed rebellion against foreign occupation prevailed in Indochina. And, each time the French quashed insurrections, they forced the Vietnamese to surrender control of their land to them. The French also participated in wars between rival Vietnamese groups and, as a "reward" from the winning faction, the French demanded more land and the right to sell French goods in trade arrangements.

Eventually, local Vietnamese leaders were replaced by French nationals. By 1925, five-thousand Frenchmen ruled over a country of 30 million. France would go on to extend control in Laos, North and South Vietnam and Cambodia, collectively called Indochina.

"Civilization Francais"

The term *"civilization Francais"* reflected French pride, if not conceit, in each aspect of life in society, from language, religion, literature, poetry and music, as well as in government, laws, educational systems and technological advancements. The goal of French colonization, particularly in Indochina, was to spread French civilization to "inferior" native peoples.

France did, in fact, modernize its Indochina colonies by

bringing electricity to Vietnam; by building public parks, hotels, restaurants and broad boulevards which resembled those in Paris. It created a law school and medical school which introduced practices of modern law and medicine. Most notably, France built railroads. The most expansive railroad connected the northern capital, Hanoi, with Saigon, the largest city in South Vietnam.

The strict Vietnamese legal system was replaced by the famous Napoleonic Codes of 1804. This French civil code banned privileges based on birth, allowed freedom of religion and declared that government jobs were to be given to the most qualified. The Code was a clearly written and publicly accessible law which the French had successfully imposed in their colonial holdings, where scattered feudal law had previously prevailed.

Economics

In 1897, France dispatched politician Paul Doumer to govern Indochina. His main mission was to generate large amounts of money to replace what France had expended in creating its Indochinese Empire. Doumer was to put Indochina on a "paying basis", by providing a market for French goods and by making profitable investments accessible to French businessmen.

To raise funds, Doumer's strategy was to encourage wide use of opium, which had previously only been confined to a small sector of the Chinese population. This single act would have far reaching consequences, as the numbers of addicted Vietnamese shot up dramatically, thus reducing a healthy quality of life. Doumer then leveled a tax on opium which supplied approximately 1/3 of the revenue needed to govern Indochina. The wine, rubber and salt trades were also heavily taxed. Those who could not or would not pay taxes lost their houses, their land, and were forced to become day laborers.

To keep Vietnam's rice trade alive and profitable, the French took over parcels of land that had been confiscated for non-payment of taxes and hired poor farmers to plant and harvest rice. Despite the increase in rice production and ensuing revenue, workers were not paid enough and could not even afford to buy food for their families. (5)

Ho Chi Minh

Armed resistance to French rule continued throughout its colonial period. Ongoing rebellions were, in large part, spearheaded by Communist groups. (6) Vietnamese revolutionary, Ho Chi Minh (1890-1969), founded the Revolutionary Youth League in 1925, which later became the Vietnamese Communist Party in 1930. Beginning in 1941, he led the Vietnamese independence movement, establishing the Democratic Republic of Vietnam in 1945. He was prime minister (1945-1955) and president (1945-1969) of the Democratic Republic of Vietnam. After the Vietnam War, the capital of the Democratic Republic of Vietnam—Saigon—was renamed Ho Chí Minh City. (7)

The Struggle to Control Vietnam Continues

As World War II got underway in 1940, Germany went on to defeat France. Taking advantage of what it considered French vulnerability, Japan convinced the French government to allow Japanese troops to occupy French Indo-China, while leaving the French government in place. Vietnamese Communists (the Viet Minh) subsequently fought the Japanese and took control of parts of northern Vietnam. By March of 1945, Japan seized control, but after its surrender in August of 1945, Ho Chi Minh and his forces resumed control, once again, in most of Vietnam. On September 2, 1945, he declared Vietnam's independence.

A Map of Moving Parts

It is no surprise that world powers ignored Vietnam's declared independence. Yet, according to the Potsdam Conference (Potsdam Agreement) held in Germany in 1945, the assembled group of Allied Chiefs of Staff partitioned Vietnam at the 16th parallel, just north of Da Nang, for geographical and strategic operational reasons.

It was further agreed that Britain would absorb the surrendering Japanese forces in Saigon and the *southern* half of Indochina, while Japanese troops in the *north* would surrender to the Chinese.

France wasted no time in sending its troops to South Vietnam to wrest control from the British. Chinese troops moved into the north. Ho Chi Minh decided to sign a treaty with France (perhaps considering it the lesser of two evils) which would replace troops in Vietnam for a period of five years. In return, France vowed to recognize Vietnam as a "free state".

Ho Chi Minh founded the Vietnamese Community Party in 1930. He would remain the leader and president of North Vietnam until his death in 1969.

The French soon reneged on their promise for statehood and fighting resumed in what became a brutal "guerrilla war". It lasted for eight long years and in 1954 ended deep in the hills of Northwestern Vietnam at a place called Dien Bien Phu. (8)

CHAPTER THREE

John P. Davis

September 20, 1934-July 21, 1965

"John was the first person to die from Holley. Over the years, seven more Holley boys died from the war. I couldn't believe it. I knew most of them."

~ *Anne Martin, John's sister*

OUR FAMILY ROOTS GO LONG AND DEEP in the Holley community, beginning with my grandfather and his job as a street car conductor in Rochester at the turn of the century. He loved it! We were told he took his task of shuttling all kinds of people in and out of and around the city very seriously. Imagine getting to know all the regular passengers by sight, and then maybe wondering why one of them wasn't on board on a particular day or on a different day than usual. He had to know every part of the city and was the perfect guy to ask for directions, or if a certain trolley would get them where they wanted to go.

I'm sure he treated them all with good humor and respect. He was well-known and well-liked. Serving others is something that seemed to run in our family. Doing something good . . . or brave . . . or necessary for the greater good of all gave members of my family a certain pride and feeling of accomplishment. We were serving a purpose.

Our father was driven in a similar way. At 15, he lied about his age because he wanted to join the army. He served in the Second

World War. After the war, he became a heavy equipment operator. But one big dream came true when he finally retired. All his life, he wanted to live near the Erie Canal, and so he moved to Holley.

John

John also felt the need to be of service and to help people. My brother did well in groups and teams. In fact, he was the first student from Holley High to work for the Holley Volunteer Fire Department. He enjoyed his work there as part of a very good team. John played soccer, baseball and basketball and really liked to hunt. Together with his volunteer buddies, he went to several fire department tournaments and built a real camaraderie.

John Davis is shown here (middle row second from left) in a team soccer photo. He was the first student from Holley to work for the town's volunteer fire department.

He was older than the other Holley boys when he went to Vietnam. In addition, he was married and had three children. But, like our father, he felt that he should serve our country and enlisted in the army. He even thought about making a career of it. He particularly liked being stationed in Germany and if it didn't mean uprooting his entire family, I often wondered if he'd end up living there.

Long Binh, Vietnam

John was stationed at the legendary Long Binh Army Post headquarters of the United States Army Vietnam (USARV) during the Vietnam War. This sprawling complex was located east of the Dong Nai River, about 20 miles from Saigon and

The sprawling military base at Long Binh was the headquarters for the U.S. Army during the Vietnam War. John was a supply sergeant there. He had hoped to make the army his career.

near the Bien Hoa Air Base. At times in its history, this inclusive, mammoth facility served as the largest US air base outside the continental United States.

By the middle of 1967, Long Binh was populated by nearly all of United States Army Vietnam HQ Command and other smaller army units who were stationed in Saigon. John was a supply sergeant there.

Luxuries and the "LBJ" Jail

The Long Binh Post was a unique logistics facility, not simply because of its tremendous size and the number of people it employed (60,000 in 1969), but also for the full range of services it provided for staff use.

Long Binh was something of a contained city in itself; a mini-mall by today's standards, including large restaurants and snack bars, dental clinics, and a Special Services Crafts Shop which offered classes, taught by personnel, in making a variety of hand-crafted items. It had access to a photo lab, a wood shop, a lapidary (etching stones and other natural materials), leather crafting, and silver and gold casting shops, among numerous other extension classes.

The site also included an Olympic size swimming pool, run by special services staff; basketball and tennis courts; a golf driving range; a bowling alley; laundry services and even nightclubs, featuring live music.

Long Binh existed in startling contrast to the dense, dangerous jungles and muddy, polluted rivers of Vietnam where the gruesome battles of the war were fiercely waged.

Although some might have considered John's assignment as a stroke of good luck, he would wage --- and lose --- his own individual battle, but not on the warfront.

LEPTO . . . what?

> *"I've tried to be careful when I say this, but I'm related to former President Richard Nixon. It's ironic, of course, with John going there (Vietnam) . . . and dying . . . and Nixon's involvement."*
>
> ~ ANNE MARTIN

Americans fighting in Vietnam encountered the unfamiliar at every turn. The physical geography of the country, the oppressive tropical weather, the challenging terrain and clammy jungles were the first obvious, uncomfortable differences most people had never experienced or really anticipated, no matter how many briefings or lectures they had.

Vietnam's political yo-yo history was ancient as its people struggled, then settled, then rebelled again, until any kind of peace was struck. Its language and culture was completely intact and completely foreign to American service men and women.

Social customs and the kinds of local food offered were equally as strange and off-putting as so much else in Vietnam. Americans might as well have been on a very distant planet.

When John contracted and was diagnosed with hepatitis, chances are that even American doctors weren't 100 percent sure of what they were dealing with. And so, the army notified my mother by telegram that John was suffering from the debilitating illness, hepatitis.

~

"Oh, God," she said, dropping the telegram on the kitchen table.

Mothers are perfectly allowed to think they can make their children feel better, by kissing a boo-boo, stroking their foreheads, or nursing them back to health with homemade soup and tender, loving care. Most of the time, it works. But, with John so far away and even if he was home, my mother would have no idea about making hepatitis go away.

John was the first of the Holley boys to die in Vietnam. He contracted a rare and mysterious disease initially not thought to be serious.

I had just come in from school. The house smelled good from Mom's roast chicken, already in the oven for that night's supper. I could never figure out how she got all the flavors of all the things she put in the chicken to smell so good, all at the same time.

"Hi! I'm home!"

"Mom? The chicken smells great!"

I headed for the kitchen and saw her just standing there, absolutely still, with her right hand on her lips. I let my book bag slide from my shoulder to the floor, where it landed with a small thud.

"Mom? Are you okay?" I asked.

Something was very wrong. She looked frightened.

I put my arm around her shoulders and hugged her as hard as I could. As good as the kitchen smelled, Mom always had a lovely fragrance about her; not overpowering but very "Mom". She smelled like spring flowers.

"John's sick," she said. "I just got this telegram. He has hepatitis . . . but they say they don't think it's serious. How do they know? Everything is serious over there."

I took the telegram from her and began reading. The yellow paper felt more like construction paper than regular stationery. It made the terse message seem more important, more serious.

"They probably just want you to know that he's being taken care of, Mom, right? It's good that we know. And, he's probably feeling better right *now*! He'll write and tell us all about it," I offered.

"But why would they write to say he's getting *better*?" she said. "Wouldn't they just fix him up and let him tell us in a letter?"

I didn't know what to say. She was justifiably worried. I placed the telegram on the kitchen table, where it stayed through supper until the next morning.

Mothers know.

They just know.

~

Hepatitis is nothing to fool around with. It is an inflammatory disease of the liver, caused by a virus. We take for granted what our body does to keep us healthy; and the liver stores nutrients and vitamins; it helps digestion, and helps to prevent infections by removing harmful things from the blood.

The beginning symptoms of hepatitis can feel like the flu: fever, diarrhea, vomiting, lack of appetite, fatigue, feeling achy, and more. A more severe case of this dreadful disease can result in jaundice, which produces a yellowing of the skin and the whites of the eyes.

It's simply horrible.

So is leptospirosis.

The more I had read about this disease, the more convinced I was that this is what John had all along. And, also learning what I now know about Vietnam, I can see how easy it was for this disease to grow.

Leptospirosis is also a bacterial infection of the liver, but 1,000 times worse than hepatitis. Its symptoms are like those of hepatitis: high fever, severe aches and muscle pain, chills, abdominal pain, jaundice, vomiting, diarrhea and also hemorrhages in the skin or mucous membranes.

Today, sophisticated lab tests can more readily and quickly diagnose this horrendous thing and immediately start patients on strong antibiotics and rigorous medical regimens. If left untreated or in very severe cases, leptospirosis can result in permanent kidney damage, meningitis (an inflammation of the membrane around the brain and spinal cord), liver failure, respiratory illness and even death. It affects both humans and animals.

So, how does one get it? It is transmitted through direct contact with the urine of infected animals or through contact with a urine-contaminated environment, such as water, soil and plants. Leptospirosis bacteria can be found in both wild and domestic animals, including dogs, cattle, pigs, horses and rodents, among others. Bacteria enters the human body through cuts or abrasions in the skin and through mucus membranes of the eyes, nose and mouth.

Leptospirosis is worldwide, occurring in both rural and urban areas, and in temperate and tropical climates. Vietnam's natural environment would seem to have been the perfect breeding ground for such a disease; especially for people working outdoors (in rice or sugar cane fields, for example) or with animals. Farmers are candidates for infection, along with sewer workers, dairy workers and, yes, military personnel. Swimming or wading in contaminated waters, particularly in tropical rainy seasons, increases the risk of contracting leptospirosis in epidemic proportions.

The Local "Menu"

In addition to the environmental dangers associated with the disease, the available Vietnamese food supply during the war was riddled with unlikely, yet plentiful and dangerous choices. There is just no easy way to wrap one's mind around the common practice of eating dog, rodent and monkey meat in Vietnam.

Street vendors cooked and sold their delicacies everywhere and you might have never known (or remembered) what you were really eating; especially if it was jammed inside native bread, swimming in soups of natural vegetation, or hiding in super spicy rice bowls.

Even service personnel, like those who worked at Long Binh, did sometimes venture out into the city streets. John may have contracted the disease on such an outing.

~

Just four days after my mother received the first telegram, a second one arrived, stating John had died.

CHAPTER FOUR

Battle of Dien Bien Phu

FOLLOWING THE END OF WORLD WAR II, the French turned their interest to Indochina, attracted to its abundant natural resources, particularly salt and valuable minerals. During that same time, however, a collection of small republics then part of the French Union in Indochina declared independence, taking the name the Popular Republic of Vietnam. In 1946, the French attacked them. Their leader, Ho Chi Minh organized the Viet Minh Army, and relying on guerilla warfare, declared war on France. The conflict lasted for seven years. In 1953, as peace talks were evolving, in order to strengthen his negotiating position, Ho Chi Minh made the calculated decision to wage a full assault against the French stronghold at Dien Bien Phu. It was this battle which eventually drew the United States into its war in Vietnam.

The Battle

Concerned with the increasing intensity of Ho Chi Minh's activity, the French appointed General Navarre to oversee its military operations in Indochina. A decorated veteran of the World Wars, Navarre was considered an expert in armored warfare. Using his experience, he chose to seize the valley of Dien

Bien Phu from the Viet Minh and use it as his base of operations.

Dien Bien Phu, near the border with Laos, was a valley seven miles long and three miles wide. It was bounded by a series of high peaks and hills along both sides, which spread in all directions deep into the jungle. The valley floor, nonetheless, was flat, which Navarre saw as an advantage for his tanks and armored vehicles, and ideal for flying in planes and helicopters.

The way Navarre envisioned it, the terrain would prohibit the Viet Minh from using big guns and artillery, limiting any attack to infantry with at best automatic weapons. He'd simply chew them up with ground artillery supported by superior air power to both strafe the enemy from above and keep his forces supplied with food and ammunition.

Other military strategists, however, were not convinced. In their opinion the valley was too far from the nearest French controlled airfields. Supply flights would be in danger of running out of fuel. Moreover, the space was insufficient for building runways, and in any case could easily be put out of order by enemy artillery. Without the runways, there were no means for transporting additional troops or ammunition into the valley. Finally, the plan's critics pointed out the uselessness of expending resources to control the one main road into the region from Laos while there were hundreds of smaller roads serving the same purpose.

Navarre was unmoved. In November of 1953, the French forces made their move, parachuting in. The Viet Minh, not at full force or ready to resist, resorted to guerilla tactics, most of which amounted to little more than annoyance. Within a few short months, the French constructed two airfields. However, due to the lack of building materials, most of the structures on the base were simple tin construction, and the artillery was left out in the open. Thirteen thousand troops were quickly moved in, most of which were housed in tents and bunkers.

The General, however, failed to account for the weather. The cool winter with its sporadic light rain rapidly gave way to the monsoons and torrential downpours. The valley floor quickly flooded, the water over-running the tents and bunkers. To make matters worse, the valley was slow to drain, leaving the runways inaccessible for long periods of time which bogged down the tanks.

While Navarre's forces were occupied setting up multiple defensive posts throughout the valley, the Viet Minh commander, General Giap, was moving his troops into position. Thousands of 'coolies', native bearers, were transporting dismantled guns by modified bicycles and ox-drawn carts up into the hundreds of fortified bunkers dug into the mountainside, concealed beneath the vegetation where they were again assembled by hand. Tens of thousands of artillery shells and mortars were carried into the hills in similar fashion.

Near the end of January, the Viet Minh began daily shelling of the French base, in isolated incidents with small caliber shells, intent only on raising the tension levels and wearing on the psyche of the French.

On March 13, the Viet Minh changed tactics, unleashing a continuous barrage of heavy mortars, taking out entire banks of French artillery, blockhouses, and command posts. Two French commanders were killed. When the artillery ceased, a division of Viet Minh soldiers concealed in trenches just outside the French perimeter charged. The French managed to hold them off, but took heavy casualties, counting 500 dead. The Viet Minh lost 600, but opened up considerable gaps in the perimeter.

The next morning, the Viet Minh attacked again. Concentrating their fire on the northern-most outpost, they destroyed the airfield, leaving huge craters in its surface while disabling many of the planes on the ground. Cut off from the rest of the base, the outpost was soon over-run by enemy infantry. More than 2,000 Viet Minh were killed in the effort, with only a handful of French soldiers managing to escape back towards the main base.

Only the timely arrival of French paratroopers saved the day. The Viet Minh attack was repelled. Nevertheless, the whole northern extent of the base was in enemy hands.

Nearly-surrounded by the Viet Minh and blocked from supplies and reinforcement, the French prepared for a final decisive push by General Giap. But luck had it that at that same moment, the United States had intervened politically in the Geneva negotiations. Giap's attack was put-off.

Two weeks later, the fighting resumed. Using the remaining tanks and artillery guns, the French managed to regain parts of the base. Following an especially aggressive battle, a large force of Viet Minh elite troops was beaten, forcing the demoralized infantry to retreat into the hills. Subsequent assault attempts were successfully rebuffed by French air and artillery.

Faced with some degree of mutiny by his troops, Giap changed tactics. He brought in fresh soldiers and directed them to dig tunnels to approach the French perimeter out of sight from planes overhead. The tactic worked. The French were forced into the southernmost part of the base.

The French defeat at Dien Bien Phu would not bode well for the United States.

Their position untenable, the French commander, De Castries, nevertheless refused to surrender. He ordered his forces to defend the one approach not yet in control of the enemy. With most of the air drops of supplies and ammunition falling into the hands of the Viet Minh and his position growing desperate, De Castries, through the French Foreign Minister, beseeched the Americans to come to his aid. President Eisenhower made the decision not to provide assistance.

On May 7, De Castries ordered his men to put down their arms. (1)

With the defeat of the French, the United States became more deeply involved in Indochina. By then, Ho Chi Minh and the

Viet Minh had perfected their guerilla warfare tactics and were confident any similar occupation would be defeated in the same way. Soon, what became known as the, "Second Indochina War" ensued and America would take the place of the French. (2)

The end result would be equally as catastrophic.

CHAPTER FIVE

David Case

August 14, 1945-September 16, 1965

"It was such a good newspaper route, that when David left I took it over. When I left, my brothers, Paul and Peter, took over the route."

~ *Bryan Case, David's Brother*

IT MAY HAVE BEEN THE LORD'S DAY, but Sunday mornings in Holley belonged to the industrious Case family. As the rest of the town slept, we were up at 5 a.m. to begin the work of delivering the Sunday edition of the *Democrat & Chronicle* to our neighbors. This job was, most definitely, a family affair; a very precise and busy one. We had the process down to a science, so that by 6:30 a.m. we'd be back home for Mom's eggs and bacon!

My brother David created the work ethic of a newspaper delivery boy, *par excellence*. He was so good at what he did that in 1957 he won a trip to New York City for having garnered the most subscriptions for the paper. He started his first delivery route when he was 12-years-old (the minimum age, then) and soon picked up a *second* route. He became so busy that I began to help him deliver papers on this route. I was only 10, so the route was still in David's name. During the week, we rode our bikes through Holley's neighborhoods, successfully completing our missions.

But on *Sundays* . . .

~

"Let's get a move on, kids," bellowed my dad, Edwin Case. "Those newspapers aren't gonna 'deliver themselves!"

We were a big family; six boys and one girl. Our intrepid Sunday delivery team was comprised of David, my brothers Paul and Peter, my sister Susie, who was only five, me, and Dad. My two remaining brothers were even younger than Susan and, of course, stayed home with Mom. Little did we know then, or even suspect, that our single family would literally pass the torch—or pass the *newspaper*—of paper delivery down to the very last Case family member.

David Case is shown here in his 5th grade class photo. He is in the first row, extreme right.

On Sundays, the stacks of newspapers came to us bundled into separate sections, which we had to assemble by hand. Then, there were advertisements, and flyers and leaflets to insert into the paper. The living room floor became our assembly line.

"Okay. You know what to do. David will start with the front page section," instructed Dad, "and pass it to Bryan, on his right, who will insert the food and coupon section. Pass it on to the right, so Paul can put in the advertising flyers . . . and when it's all packed, pass it on to Peter at the end to stack in piles."

Aye, aye, sir! The only thing missing was a whistle blow to start the race!

This involved a lot of work and concentration and our family operation went quite smoothly for a good six years—and this was only for the morning edition. Finally, we'd all trundle out to the family station wagon, load the papers into it, and take off with Dad at the wheel. David would deliver to one side of the street, while I did the other side.

Even Susan took part in the routine. At five-years-old, she was probably the youngest delivery girl, who learned to roll the paper up and stick it between the storm door and main door of a house. Eventually, when they were officially old enough, Paul and Susan took over a route in Case family fashion.

The Good, the Bad and the Beagles

There were valuable lessons to be learned in the paper delivery business; patience being right there at the top of the list. You see, everyone wanted their paper delivered in a particular spot at their home. Some wanted the paper left at the front door or in the milk box or in the mail box, or under the doormat, and on and on. As much as we wanted to please our neighbors, it often slowed us down.

Yet, the hardest part of delivering papers was getting paid. We provided a necessary service, and some people were very good about paying on time, or even in advance. But, there were some customers who were harder than others to catch at home; or had excuses for not having the money and some wanted us to come to collect at a specific time each week. We worked very hard trying to accommodate them. Sometimes, being compensated was even harder.

I do remember one particular morning, when I was chased by what I considered to be a *pack* of beagles! It was scary! I was a kid trying to do my job, and suddenly, there were barks and growls! I was even nipped that day and had tiny battle scars to prove it.

As much as my father took great responsibility and pride in our reliable family business, he didn't hesitate to call the beagles' owners, informing them that if they couldn't control their dogs, they wouldn't be getting the paper anymore. I don't remember another incident.

No Greater Gift

"Holley, New York Cub Scout pack 119, sponsored by Holley Central School Assn., Lewiston Trail Council, E. Duane Case re-commissioned as Cub master, Pauline Case, den mother, 7th year of scouting "Onward for God and My Country Program."

~ The Democrat and Chronicle, *September 14, 1958*

The Case family's venture into the newspaper delivery business was, of course, just one example of the way they viewed their commitment to Holley and its surrounding communities. But more than that, a sense of family strength and solidarity permeated their household and the activities they chose to pursue.

My dad served in the army during World War II. Just before the war ended, he was transferred to Indianapolis, where he met and married my mom.

David was born on the day the war ended, August 14, 1945. My mom often told us that as she was being wheeled out of the hospital delivery room, she heard a radio broadcast. A serious and familiar voice was speaking. It was President Truman announcing VJ Day in the Pacific.

Mom's story never changed. She said she smiled and said, "I had a feeling we'd have a son on a great, great day."

David was also very active in local sports and played in the Little League when Dad was its coach. But, I personally believe that when David was in the Cub Scouts and Boy Scouts—where my father was Scout Leader for many years and my mother was a Den Mother—he developed a sense of duty to God and country that never left him. I really think that his participation in the Scouts and the lessons it imparted, eventually led him to joining the Marines and ultimately volunteering to go to Vietnam.

He was just a great kid and a great brother. He was also creative. A collage he made hung in the high school principal's office until his death. Afterwards, it was given to the Davis family in Holley. Their son, John, was the first boy from Holley to die in Vietnam. David was the second. He was 20-years-old.

According to his unit commander, David was also a great Marine. The same church minister who worked with David when he earned the Scout's "God and Country Award" officiated at his funeral. "We all ought to consider ourselves his friend because no greater gift can any friend give than his life," he said.

~

One family friend, Darryl Cady, remembers going to that same church (the First Presbyterian Church), where my parents and the six of us kids would occupy the pew right in front of his parents and their six children. Darryl and I were church ushers together. In fact, we were best friends in high school. Like many of the boys, we'd go to Oak Orchard Bowling Alley in Albion for the dances and sock hops with real rock 'n roll bands. When we got older, we'd go to Brockport to meet college girls.

"I can't stand in the children's way. I believe in this."

~*Edwin Case, David's father*

I joined the Navy in 1965 right after David was killed. My brother, Paul, joined the Marines, but he wasn't allowed to serve in Vietnam because David was killed there. My brother Peter was 15 at the time and was preparing to attend one of the service academies in a military prep school.

My father was quoted in the paper as saying, "It bothered me for a little while, but the 15-year-old wants to be in the space programs, and if there's anything more dangerous than that, I don't know about it."

Operation "Starlite": By Land and By Sea

I got used to people saying, "Preston, you are one lucky guy." From 1965 through 1968, I was stationed in the Pentagon working in the war message center during the Vietnam War. It was my job to receive and transmit information considered *secret* and *top secret* from all over the world and route it to the appropriate military civilian units. It's funny, even after 50 years; I'm still sworn to secrecy about some of it. But, what happened on the evening of September 20, 1965, I *can* talk about.

When I first arrived at the Pentagon in March of 1965, the Vietnam War was still in its early stages. That, however, would begin to change by August of 1965. At that time, both American and South Vietnamese forces were quartered together inland, just off the coast of the South China Sea.

On August 15, the South Vietnamese commanding General was advised of the unexpected arrival of a 17-year-old boy, claiming to be a defector from Vietcong forces. He told the General that a large Vietcong force had gathered near their location and were preparing to attack. The Vietnamese General immediately informed the Marine commander, Lt. Gen. Lewis W. Walt.

Walt was a no-nonsense, call-to-action kind of man. He weighed his options: hold and reinforce the Marine's position to expect the attack or go on the offensive and attack the Vietcong position before they could take the initiative. Walt chose to attack.

Walt worked for two nights straight to coordinate what would become the first combined effort using both amphibious vehicles and helicopters in a combat operation. General Walt chose the name "Starlight" for the operation. However, the clerks writing up the communication documents were doing so by candle light only, as the main generators had gone out. A clerk misread the name of the operation, typing in "Starlite" instead of "Starlight".

And so, *Operation Starlite* began at sunrise in Vietnam. The Vietcong did expect the attack—from *land*, not from the sea, where Gen. Walt had secretly amassed an armada of amphibious vehicles. Two lone Vietcong soldiers were sent to the beach to lay a line of land mines in the sand and ordered to kill as many Marines as possible. The intent of the Vietcong orders was to delay the American approach, to allow Vietcong commanders to escape to more fortified locations. The two Vietcong soldiers panicked when they were faced with 30 amphibious vehicles and set off the mines, prematurely. Fortunately, the Marines suffered no casualties.

The Element of Surprise

At the same time, Marine helicopters were carrying infantry inland to multiple landing zones, west, north and south of the Vietcong. It was to be a traditional *hammer and anvil* operation, in which forces coming from the sea would drive the enemy towards those forces waiting to cut off their escape.

When confronted by American troops, it was characteristic for the Vietcong to recede and vanish into the jungle. First Lt. Mike Jenkins, commanding a portion of the ground troops, set his eye on routing the Vietcong from neighboring villages. What appeared to be simple huts were actually reinforced bunkers which housed heavily armed Vietcong fighters. Jenkins' troops withstood heavy fire, and retreated. He struck a second time, focusing on one target at a time, then another and successfully took a hill above this target(s). From this vantage point, Jenkins began an assault on the village below. As they made their approach, they were outflanked by a large Vietcong force, camouflaged as natural terrain. Jenkins and his men may have lost their position and their lives at that moment, had it not been for the efforts of Lance Corporal Ernie Wallace, who was armed with a machine gun. Singlehandedly, Wallace attacked the Vietcong, killing 25.

Jenkins' troops proceeded down the hill, while squad leader, Cpl. Dick Tonucci, assumed a machine gun position and pinned down the Vietcong long enough for Jenkins' men to advance.

The Vietcong by then had strengthened their ground, ultimately forcing Jenkins' troop to retreat to the landing zone. Only 28 men survived the attack.

The Human Spoils of War

The concurrent amphibious attack against Vietcong in a small, rural village was led by a Captain Webb and India Company, after permission was granted for his sea forces to continue on land. Webb's goal was to have a section of tanks find a way around a non-traversable trench to reach the enemy's stronghold. The attack on the village ensued, driving off or killing Vietcong soldiers. Staff Sergeant Jean Pinguet was making sure the downed Vietcong were, in fact, dead, by shooting rounds into their heads as they lay on the field. Capt. Webb ordered him to stop out of respect. At that moment, a grenade was flung from the hand of one of the wounded Vietcong soldiers who was pretending to be dead. Webb was killed instantly.

The tank battalion squad leader, Corporal Robert O'Malley, engaged in hand-to-hand combat with the Vietcong. He and Lance Corporal Chris Buchs jumped into a Vietcong trench, a stronghold, and eliminated eight soldiers before they could reload their weapons. For his actions, O'Malley was the first Marine in Vietnam to be awarded the Medal of Honor for heroism.

Subsequently, the American supply line from the beach attempted to deliver munitions to O'Malley. They were attacked en route. This attack disabled and stalled both lead and rear vehicles in the convoy. The Vietcong fired, but Lt. Robert Cochran managed to hold off the enemy into the night.

Colonel Peatross ordered India Company to the rescue. They, too, were ambushed and the mission was aborted. Peatross ordered the supply chain to dig in for the night and wait for help to arrive. From above, helicopters continued to strafe (fly over the location and spray with ammunition) the nearby jungle by night. The remaining Vietcong fled into the jungle; 600 had died. The Americans lost 52 Marines.

~

After this confrontation in the jungle, remaining Vietcong forces proceeded to a stronghold on a peninsula further north. Marines began an air assault by helicopter, locating Vietcong soldiers in a series of well-entrenched caves. This operation lasted three days. One-hundred-seventy-eight Vietcong soldiers were killed; 360 were taken as prisoners. However, local villagers informed the Marines that a much larger force of Vietcong soldiers had escaped before their arrival.

A few days after *Operation Piranha,* Marine infantry were sent to the same location to *sweep* for remaining Vietcong. One of the amphibious tractors—*"amtracs"*—hit a land mine. The dead and wounded were removed. Yet, to protect the disabled vehicle from interference by the enemy, a second amtrac was dispatched to guard the first one. That second vehicle also hit a land mine en route to the first vehicle. Two Marines were killed.

A Dreadful Discovery

"What I saw haunts me to this very day."

In my opinion, that last maneuver should have been the end of *Operation Starlite*. Tragically, that was not to be.

On the following evening, September 20, I was working a routine shift at the Pentagon. A fellow worker called me over to her desk to help with a particular problem. As we were working to correct it, I happened to glance down at her teletype machine. What I saw haunts me to this very day. It was a notice advising that David D. Case had been killed in Vietnam the day before.

I was shocked into absolute silence. I was numb.

Not only did David and I go to Holley High School together; he was also my neighbor. We were in the Boy Scouts together back home and David's parents were our scout leaders. To this day, I contemplate the odds of this event.

David couldn't have been in Vietnam for more than two weeks. He was a victim of the very first battle in the Vietnam War, which I have recounted.

He was the second boy from Holley to die during the war. So many, too many.

I knew and grew up with most of the local boys killed in Vietnam. John Davis lived across the street from me. George Fischer was one of my best friends. I was in the school marching band with George and Ronnie Sisson. And, I knew Gary Stymus, Howard Bowen and Gary Bullock.

May they rest in peace.

David was the second boy from Holley to die in Vietnam. His personnel carrier hit a land mine during operation Starlite.

"To this day, I contemplate the odds of this event."

~ LOREN PRESTON, DAVID'S CLASSMATE AND NEIGHBOR

Thank You for Your Service

Eight young men from Holley lost their lives in the Vietnam War. Orleans County officials believed that toll to be higher than any other community of its size (population approximately 1,800 in 1973) in the nation.

Cletus Buelte, a former foreman at Rochester Taylor Instrument Company; a onetime amateur softball and semi-pro baseball player, and Commissioner, Scout Master and Assistant Scout Master in the Lewiston Trail Council of Boy Scouts, said, "I knew three of the boys very well—Gary Bullock, David Case and Gary Stymus. They were in my Scout Troop."

Buelte was 73 in 1973. He strongly believed in and displayed his dedication to these boys—and all veterans of war—by religiously placing staffed American flags on their graves. They were hard to forget, especially since Buelte's home on South Holley Road bordered Hillside and Holy Cross Cemeteries. He firmly felt that it was the obligation of Holley to honor these men.

He also decorated the graves at Sandy Creek Cemetery on West Ridge Road, which encompassed the graves of those who perished in the Spanish-American War, the Revolutionary War, the Civil War, World War I, World War II, and the Korean and Vietnam Wars.

Buelte said it was a "voluntary job", but something he could contribute to in his retirement. *

All of the Vietnam graves sit in a special plot in Hillside Cemetery. "We owe them so much," said Buelte.

Remembering David

Mrs. Case requested that her son, David, be buried in Woodlawn National Cemetery in Elmira, New York. The Case family makes the 130-mile trip four times a year to visit his grave.

Mr. Case agreed upon the site of his son's interment, mostly because he felt his wife couldn't have endured driving past the Holley cemetery every time she traveled, if David was laid to rest there.

> *"I'm glad the war is over. I hope those who gave their lives have not died in vain."*
>
> ~MRS. EDWIN D. CASE, DAVID'S MOTHER, 1973

CHAPTER SIX

Diem Assassination

FOR AMERICANS, 1963 will forever be associated with the assassination of President John F. Kennedy. For others however, it is the year in which, only weeks prior, Ngo Dinh Diem, the president of South Vietnam, along with his brother, Ngo Dinh Nhu, his chief advisor, were both assassinated. Historically, these events are inexorably linked together.

Following the defeat of the French in 1954 at the hands of Ho Chi Minh and the Viet Minh, Vietnam was divided into two parts. Everything south of the 17th parallel was declared the State of South Vietnam. Everything to the north remained the People's Republic of North Vietnam. The arrangements were meant to be temporary until the South Vietnamese government could properly establish itself and elections could be held. Once that was accomplished, it was believed, the nation could again become unified.

To establish that government, the former Emperor, at the time serving as the head of state, named Diem the Prime Minister. He was intended to hold the position until national elections could be held in 1956. However, prior to the scheduled elections, Diem proposed the formation of the Republic of Vietnam. He then proceeded to rig the process, declaring himself president of the new nation. To strengthen his legitimacy, he formed the Army of the Republic of Viet Nam, and used it to enforce his policies. Dissident voices were

Ngo Dinh Diem, the President of South Vietnam, is shown reviewing ARVN troops. His assassination drew the United States deeper into the Vietnam War.

accused of conspiring with the Viet Cong, and those people were put to death. To further assure loyalty, key government positions were given to his brother, in-laws, and to Catholics of influence. At the time, the Roman Catholic Church was the largest land owner in Vietnam. Diem was a devout Catholic.

Over the next nine years, Diem ruled with an iron fist, but not without serious challenges. In 1960, a coup attempt by his own officers discontented with the favoritism shown to the Catholics among their ranks, mainly in the form of promotion, was foiled by troops loyal to the president. Later, in 1962, two pilots from the ARVN paratrooper division flew over Diem's palace and dropped bombs. Though the palace suffered extensive damage, Diem again managed to escape with his life.

Protest

The final straw, however, came in 1963. Diem's brother had been consecrated as Archbishop of the church. In celebration, Diem outlawed the Buddhist flag, and in its place hung the Vatican Flag. A group of Buddhist priests protested. Nine of them were gunned down by the ARVN and Diem's police. Later that summer, forces under the direction of Diem's brother conducted coordinated raids on Buddhist temples throughout the country. Thousands of monks were arrested, hundreds more died.

Early in 1963, concerned with the turmoil in South Vietnam, President John F. Kennedy dispatched Henry Cabot Lodge to serve as Ambassador. There are theories that Lodge, impatient with Diem, whom he considered inept and corrupt, may have contributed covertly to further the ambitions of those set on removing Diem and his brother from power. (1)

Regardless, on November 1, Diem's Military Advisor and his Army Chief of Staff, backed by a large number of rebel ARVN forces, blocked all main roads into Saigon and surrounded the presidential palace. With only Diem's Presidential Guards to offer resistance, the palace was quickly taken. Diem agreed to surrender.

While the leaders of the coup were meeting to decide their next step, Diem and his brother used the opportunity to flee the palace. Diem had previously ordered the construction of three secret tunnels leading out into the thick jungle surrounding the palace. Together, they fled to a friend's house where they attempted to gain asylum in China. The Chinese denied their request. Shortly thereafter, Diem made a phone call to Lodge.

Coup

Only days earlier, Lodge, believing that a takeover of the government was imminent, had alerted Kennedy, requesting in advance a plane to fly the Diem brothers out of Vietnam. President Kennedy, however, did not want the United States associated with the coup. A pre-arranged flight would have suggested nothing less.

After taking the call from Diem, according to Colonel Mike Dunn, Lodge's aide at the time, Lodge put Diem on hold and left the room. When he returned, Lodge informed Diem that he would not be able to arrange the agreed upon flight to the Philippines until the next day. Dunn believed it was a delay tactic, and that when Lodge left the room it was to tell the coup leaders where Diem could be found. Interestingly enough, it was Lodge who convinced Diem not to resist the coup attempt.

Dunn, hoping to circumvent the assassination, offered to Lodge to go along with the Diem brothers for the formal surrender. Lodge turned him down, stating that the presence of an American would be interpreted as United States involvement in and support of the coup.

The next day, the coup leaders tracked Diem and his brother to the church of St. Francis Xavier. At approximately ten that morning, the President and his brother were arrested. They were transported in an armored vehicle back towards military headquarters. Along the way, Diem's brother and the captain overseeing the escort began to exchange insults. Suddenly and without warning, the captain attacked Nhu with a bayonet, stabbing him over and over again. He stopped only long enough to pull out a pistol and shoot the president once in the head. He then turned his weapon on Nhu, who by then had collapsed to the floor of the vehicle, and he shot him multiple times. Photos which were later leaked showed both men had their hands tied. (2)

Following news of the assassination, Lodge suggested to Kennedy, furthering the lies told by the Viet Nam news media, that the Diem brothers had committed suicide by ingesting poison. Not believing that such devout Catholics would commit suicide, and especially at a church, Kennedy ordered Lucien Conein, the CIA contact with the ARVN, to find the Diems' bodies. Conein confronted Minh, the coup leader, with the truth. With the assassination confirmed, Conein, in order to maintain deniability, rejected the opportunity to see the bodies.

Kennedy was later to take responsibility for approving measures encouraging Lodge to explore potential coup attempts. He insisted, however, that the plan was always to provide asylum to Diem and his brother, as long as it could be done without a chance of Diem ever returning to power in Viet Nam.

Nevertheless, the death of Diem created a leadership vacuum

exploited by the Viet Cong, who infiltrated the South and sowed the seeds of discontent. (3)

History is clear on what happened next.

CHAPTER SEVEN

Ronald P. Sisson

October 26, 1942–December 16, 1965

"No evil can happen to a good man, either in life or after death."

~ *Ronald Sisson's high school senior photo caption*

December 16, 1965
Quang Tin Province
17:30 hours

Ronald Sisson

We shouldn't be here. Not two nights in a row. It's standard operating procedure to keep moving and not spend a second night in the same location. Way too easy for the enemy to calibrate your position. We were taught to have your next night's location planned even as you were hunkering down the night before. Hell, it made sense. But the South Vietnamese Army commander was either too arrogant, too stupid or both. Our Sergeant complained but he couldn't change his mind, now.

We returned to our patrol base which we established on yet another one of Vietnam's endless hills. I climbed so many I thought maybe I should have been a mountain goat or mule. It's too bad there's a war going on. Parts of this country are pretty as a picture.

Next to me is Cpl. Raymond Joy from Texas. He has a funny

way of talking, but he's a real nice guy. That's one thing about Nam; you find yourself with people you would have never met otherwise. Like C.D., who I met in Camp Pendleton. He's in our unit but on another mission tonight. We became friends in Camp Hanson on the way over.

No one knows what the next day will bring. It's kind of exciting, but I think that when this war is over I'll have had enough excitement to last a lifetime. We've been humping all day and observed several armed enemy troops in the area and located several staging areas and supply camps. The NVA are all over the place. All the more reason to 'de-de' out of here and report our findings. But now we're forced to make camp on this same hill for a second night.

We spend the next hour establishing our night defensive position, setting out claymores, trip flares, and listening posts; then we wolf down some chow and make some coffee. Never drank the stuff until I came here. Before it's too dark I have just enough time to write this short letter home wishing everyone a merry Christmas, which is just a week away.

Although it's December it is still warm here during the day but cold and wet at night. Not like home in December. I sure do miss the snow; bet there's a foot on the ground already. Somehow we always managed to have a real jim-dandy Christmas, we are so much more fortunate than most kids in town when it comes to good times.

I wrote Mom and Dad that I received their Christmas goodies. Although by the time they were delivered to me out in the bush, they were flat as a pancake. Looked like an elephant sat on them! I shared them with my buddies. They sure went fast.

I told Mom and Dad not to worry. I enclosed $100 in the envelope to give my brothers and sister a real nice Christmas. I wrote that although I wouldn't be there this year, you can bet your life I'll be there in my dreams.

Gosh, I wish I was home in Holley…

Well Remembered, Well Loved

"He never had a bad word to say about anyone, or anything.

"Ron and I were deployed together to Vietnam from Camp Pendleton as part of a small detachment from 1st Force Recon. We sailed over on the USS Valley Forge in June 1965 to Okinawa. While in Okinawa, Ron gave me his 'Hot Dog Jacket', which was a Marine bomber jacket and a sports jacket to keep in my sea bag. I guess his was too full to hold them. Our bags were stored in Okinawa while we went to Vietnam with the intentions of picking them (back) up when we left.

"Suffice (it)to say Ron never made it back. I kept his clothes in my sea bag when I returned to the States not really knowing what to do with them. After forty years I was reminiscing about my 'Nam days and remembered that Ron was from upstate New York and by luck (I)tracked down the town he was from; and from there (I)contacted Don, his brother. I then had the pleasure of meeting Don when he came to California. It was there I gave him Ron's 'Hot Dog Jacket'."

~ *Charles "C.D." Smith, Ronald's Marine buddy in Vietnam*

~

"Your death ended my life of innocence. It brought the war into my world.

"I remember the night that we were at drum corps practice when they announced you had been killed. It seemed like you had just been home playing with the corps. I will never forget the emptiness in my stomach as they told us. I ended up in Vietnam a couple of years later. There were more of our friends that followed you but your death changed my life."

~ *Duane Good, Classmate and friend*

Ronald Sisson, extreme left, is shown here in a student council photo. He is in the first row, second from the right. He was active in all aspects of student life.

He Made a Great Town Even Better

"I think the entire town thought Holley was special. I think this created a culture of pride and exceptionalism.

"Ron was very charismatic. He lit up a room when he walked in. I loved him. He was a wonderful friend. One time he wrote me from Vietnam to help him enlist others to collect clothes for the Vietnamese children because they were so poor. That was the way he was. He always helped others.

"He had a lovely voice. We would always go caroling at Christmas time and sing for the home-bound and the elderly. His family was very poor. In fact, none of us were rich. We all wore the same clothes, did the same things, drove the same cars. His family might have been poor, but that never stopped him from achieving things.

"One thing I'll never forget was when the Holley marching band returned from the state championships. The band didn't arrive back in town until midnight yet the whole town had turned out and actually held a parade for the band! The parents and teachers would have bake sales and other fund raisers in order*

to have all the band members have nice uniforms and money to travel. I think this created a culture of pride and exceptionalism.

"The town had great pride, especially after the school marching band became so successful and won all of those state championships.

"Another thing that I think set Holley apart from the other towns was our church and the school choir and the school plays. We always wanted to be better than the other towns. The Methodist Church in town set the standard. Ron was a member of the Methodist Youth Fellowship. Everyone in town attended church."

~ *Janice Stedman, Classmate and friend*

'Ronnie' Sisson in a rare photo, seen performing in the school play, "Oklahoma". Standing with his foot on a box is George Fischer Jr., another boy from Holley who died in Vietnam.

Taking Care of People: A Brother and a Friend

"Ron was a member of the school band, played the clarinet, sang in the adult choir; was a volunteer fireman for the town, a member of the Young Men's Republican Club, worked for Eastman Kodak, and was a member of the student council."

~ DONALD SISSON, BROTHER

"I Would Do Anything for Him"

"My brother Ron was about six years older than me. Therefore, I looked up to him with fondness and respect. He earned it completely. He was very charismatic. Everyone liked him because he was funny, but mostly he was kind and giving. My earliest memory of his thoughtful nature was when I was very young he bought me a bow and arrow. He not only bought me things but spent time with me, too. He always took me to Rochester Red Wings games.

"Due to my admiration and love for him, I would do anything for him. An example of this is when the milk truck would come on Tuesdays, Ron would love to get buttermilk and offer me some. Well, I didn't want to disappoint him, so I would choke down the buttermilk and pretend to like it.

"He was a very sensitive man. When the teachers failed me in the seventh grade, Ron talked to the teachers and convinced them to move me to the eighth grade. So as not to disappoint him, I made the honor role that year.

"He was always the kind of guy who tried hard at everything. When we were in marching band together, I remember he would march bringing his legs higher than normal so as to do his very best. It was exhausting but he never relaxed his legs.

"He was always happy and loved to sing.

"The last thing I remember is that he took the time to write me when he was in the Marines. His letters were always upbeat.

He found good in the country and the people.

"I miss him dearly."

~JIM SISSON, BROTHER

After Action Report

"The 1st Force Recon Company was to be inserted into an area near Hill 508 in Quang Tin Province, establish a base camp, and conduct patrols in an effort to locate a regimental HQ of the 325th NVA Division. The forces departed at 0530, 14 Dec 1965, the base camp was established atop a hill, and three recon teams began their work in the area. The teams spotted a number of armed enemy troops and located several staging and supply camps but avoided any engagements with the enemy. By 1730, 16 Dec, the recon teams had returned to their base camp and began preparations to return to headquarters.

Ronnie Sisson shown in his Marine dress blues was posthumously awarded the Silver Star for valor. He died as he had lived, helping and saving others.

"At about 1900 two mortar rounds landed on the north side of the hill - but that was only the beginning of a vicious mortar attack accompanied by a ground assault by 150-200 Vietcong and North Vietnamese troops. The friendly force was unable to establish a coherent defensive perimeter and lacked sufficient manpower to both defend the portions of the hill still held and counter-attack the areas captured by the VC/NVA. When it became apparent that the hilltop could not be held, the allied force broke into small groups and withdrew into the surrounding jungle with the intent of evading back to base.

Ronnie Sisson, seen facing the camera, soon after arriving in Vietnam. According to one of his Marine Vietnam buddies, "Ronnie was a great guy, very decent, never had a bad word to say about anything or anyone".

"The withdrawing troops dribbled into the Special Forces Camp throughout 17 and 18 Dec. By the 19th there were 25 men still missing - 4 Marines, 1 Special Forces sergeant, and 20 CIDG troops. At first light on 21 December a force of 7 Marines, 4 Army Special Forces troops, 3 Australians, and 120 indigenous troops departed to search for those still missing. The recovery effort was not opposed and 14 bodies were located. Among the Americans killed was LCPL Ronald P. Sisson from Holley, New York."

Silver Star

The President of the United States of America takes pride in presenting the Silver Star (Posthumously) to Lance Corporal Ronald P. Sisson, United States Marine Corps, for conspicuous gallantry and intrepidity in action during reconnaissance operations while serving as a communicator with Second Platoon, First Force Reconnaissance Company, Third Reconnaissance Battalion, THIRD Marine Division, deep in Viet Cong territory in the Republic of Vietnam on the night of 16 December 1965. When the patrol base from which Corporal Sisson's reconnaissance team was working came under heavy Viet Cong attack, he exhibited uncommon courage in an attempt to establish radio communications with the base camp and subjected himself to intense and exacting enemy fire. When the Viet Cong force of approximately three hundred assaulted the patrol base, the defenders were forced to maneuver to a secure position. Corporal Sisson, though wounded in the leg, began dragging another wounded comrade to safety when he was killed. By his heroic conduct and selfless devotion to duty he upheld the highest traditions of the Marine Corps and the United States Naval Service. He gallantly gave his life in the cause of freedom.

> I cannot even imagine the heartache our mother went through.
>
> ~*Linda Johnson, Sister*

My mother told a reporter from the Democrat & Chronicle that Ron "wanted to fight so his brothers wouldn't have to" and that "he believed in what he was there for."

We weren't notified of his death (December 16, 1965) until after Christmas. The presents and letters we sent him were returned to us, unopened. Included in the package was a note from the Pentagon informing us of his death.

~

Ron was born two months prematurely. He was not thriving in the hospital so my mother signed him out and put him on her own special formula. He not only thrived . . . but he was the biggest and strongest of all her eight children. Ironically he was killed on the day he should have been born.

Our mother was very close to Ron. I remember her talking about a time that they had an argument before he deployed. He said he was sorry and hugged her tightly. That would have been my brother, always very conscientious and loving. After he died she said that she could still feel his arms around her waist. That always stayed with me. I cannot even imagine the heartache our mother went through.

He was so kind and concerned.

Ron was a very caring person; not just for family, but for other neighbors as well. He would check in on the elderly to see how they were doing. And, once he bought a lamp so one of the seniors could read their mail.

When I was about 16, I became very ill and Ronnie would carry me downstairs to the bathroom and back up to my room. He did this for an entire two weeks. He was so kind and concerned.

Going Home

Our little church had never seen such a gathering. There, brought together by deep grief and personal loss, were all those touched by the charm that was uniquely Ronnie's.

Family, relatives, firemen, police, teachers, school officials, village dignitaries, fellow workers, students, neighbors, business people, veterans---they were all there, his community in cross section. All eyes were upon the flag draped casket before the pulpit. To one side was a large floral tribute with "United States Marine Corps" lettered on it. This caught one's attention. But, the smaller floral basket, proclaiming simply the word, "Son", provoked the more painfully sharp stab of emotion from our family and the onlookers.

In the background, the white-haired organist, Mrs. Johnson, softly played the songs he loved. She rendered them almost as a lullaby, and the hush was broken only by mom's occasional sob. "The Lord's Prayer", "Danny Boy", "Smiling Through", and startling, "Silent Night" --- these Ronnie had sung; the last one he had mentioned hearing on the radio while writing his last letter home the night he died.

Hillside Cemetery where Ronnie Sisson is buried along with three other Holley boys.

The six Marines who would act as an honorary firing squad moved out before the casket, followed by the pall bearers, their faces reflecting the emotions of all who watched. Behind them came the two honor guards, and the church slowly emptied. From the organ came a haunting farewell, "The Marine Hymn".

Outside, in the cold January afternoon, knots of people looked on as the hearse and procession moved through the streets. At the cemetery, a crowd had gathered near the gravesite. Silent words of faith and prayer marked the brief ceremony. As the sad, sweet refrain of "Taps" rolled across the snow-white glade, the honor guards moved swiftly to the casket, removed the flag and deftly folded it into a triangle. It was passed to our mother (who was) quietly crying nearest the grave. She clutched it to her breast and haltingly walked away, stopping just once to glance back. She was followed to her car by the Marine guard, who assisted her in, and spoke briefly to her. The car pulled away. She was still clutching the flag, burying her face in it.

The snow was falling more heavily as the crowd made its way out of the cemetery.

Our brother, Ronnie, had come home.

~Linda Johnson, Sister

CHAPTER EIGHT

Gulf of Tonkin

THE ASSASSINATION OF NGO DINH DIEM opened the door for the United States' entrance into a war in Viet Nam. The incident in the Gulf of Tonkin pushed it through.

Following the death of Diem, the government leaders succeeding him were viewed as weak and incompetent—both by Washington and the North Vietnamese. While Washington chose a neutral position—at least on the surface, the Viet Minh worked at infiltrating the South and creating unrest. As tensions grew and the Viet Minh became more of a threat, the Americans under newly sworn in President Lyndon B. Johnson (JFK had recently been assassinated) were concerned that Russian interest in and support of Ho Chi Minh would strengthen Russia's presence in Indochina. So the US began a campaign to goad the North Vietnamese into an armed conflict. The incident in the Gulf of Tonkin was the first step.

In early 1964, South Vietnam, in response to the hostilities perceived on the part of the North, initiated a series of commando raids and intelligence gathering missions along the coastline east of Hanoi. They weren't very successful, more often than not leading to ARVN casualties and loss of equipment and arms.

In response, William C. Moreland, then commander of MACV-SOG, suggested the use of South Vietnamese patrol boats, and instead of making inland sorties with soldiers, begin hitting strategic positions with shells and mortars.

At the same time, the United States Navy deployed destroyers to conduct reconnaissance and information gathering further out in the Tonkin Gulf in international waters. As part of their mission, they sought out information that would help the South Vietnamese detect North Vietnamese patrol boats. (1)

On July 28, the destroyer *USS Maddox* was on patrol in the Gulf at the same time the South Vietnamese patrol boats were conducting attacks on Viet Cong radar positions. The destroyer remained in the location long enough to observe North Vietnamese torpedo boats in pursuit of the South Vietnamese. The commander of the *Maddox* ordered the destroyer out of the area. When later queried by his superiors as to the incident, the commander denied having any knowledge of the attack or the pursuit.

The Gulf of Tonkin incident which may never have even occurred, led to a Congressional resolution allowing Lyndon Johnson to lead the nation into war.

Only a few days later, the *Maddox* returned to those waters. Its presence was detected by the North Vietnamese. Hoping to avoid confrontation, Captain Herrick, the commander, again ordered the ship out to sea. For some reason, he then ordered the ship to reverse course and move towards one of the islands attacked that previous evening. Three North Vietnamese torpedo boats were sent out in response.

The Attack?

At the point the torpedo boats neared the perimeter of hostile intent, the *Maddox* fired three shots over the bow of the nearest boat. The boat responded by firing off a torpedo, and then another. A second boat then fired two more torpedos. All four missed the *Maddox*. The first torpedo boat then opened fire with its guns, a single shell piercing the *Maddox* with no effect.

Captain Herrick responded by ordering the *USS Maddox* to bring its guns to bear upon the torpedo boats. At the same time, air support was called in from the nearby *USS Ticonderoga*. The first North Vietnamese boat took heavy damage. All three then turned and fled. From above, the four fighter jets from the *Ticonderoga* strafed the patrol boats leaving one of the boats dead in the water and on fire. The remaining two were left to limp towards their base.

Informed of the incident, President Johnson ordered the *Maddox* to return to the Gulf the next day. He was intent on establishing the legitimacy of a US presence in international waters, and to show that the US would not be intimidated.

That same night, the South Vietnamese resumed their attacks on Viet Cong positions along the coast. A security garrison was attacked at the mouth of the Ron River, and another radar transmitting site was destroyed. In all, the South fired almost 800 shells in the two sorties. The simultaneous presence of the *Maddox* was seen by the Viet Cong as US support of the South Vietnamese.

Shortly after these attacks, the *Maddox* intercepted Viet Cong communications suggesting a direct attack on it by a new wave of torpedo boats. Unlike that previous night, however, the weather was marked by strong storms, poor visibility, and high seas.

Sometime during the night, the *Maddox* detected a radar presence it thought to be enemy vessels. The attack, or so it seemed, was coming from all directions, the blips appearing and disappearing. There were reports of automatic weapons fire, the launch of at least 20 torpedoes, sightings of torpedo wakes, and even the lights of enemy ships. Captain Herrick responded by pointing his guns in the direction of the blips and firing almost 400 rounds.

At this same time, Commander Stockdale from the *USS Ticonderoga* had taken off in a fighter jet to lend support. After flying over the area, from where he stated he had a clear view, he determined that the *Maddox* was firing on phantom boats. There were no enemy vessels in the area. Herrick responded by sending a message via Honolulu to Washington. He acknowledged that there was no attack, blaming the weather for the anomalies on the radar.

Unfortunately, only hours after his first message, Herrick sent another in which he assured Secretary of Defense Robert McNamara that the attacks were bona fide. Although doubts remained, it was enough for President Johnson to address the American people, and in essence, declare war on the North Vietnamese, stating that "repeated acts of violence against the armed forces of the United States…must be met with positive reply" (Peterson 2008). That reply was an all-out assault by 18 fighter jets off the *USS Ticonderoga* on a fuel storage facility at Vinh. The depot was leveled and all vessels destroyed. Two of the fighter jets were downed. One of the pilots was killed, the other was taken prisoner. (2)

On August 7, following the convening of an emergency session of Congress, the President asked for and was granted the authorization to unilaterally use military force against any perceived aggression against the United States. Called the Gulf of Tonkin Resolution, the measure—based on an event which probably never occurred—encouraged LBJ to escalate the campaign in Viet Nam.

CHAPTER NINE

Howard L. Bowen

April 9, 1946-November 8, 1966

IT WAS ALMOST LIKE A FIRE DRILL IN MY HOUSE. The process of de-skunking that is. My brother was always into something in the great outdoors. We were raised on a farm and being around animals just came naturally. But, this boy had a penchant for encounters with skunks!

Mom was always ready-at-the-pump with a horde of canned tomato juice in the pantry for undoing the horrendous stench that trailed Howie everywhere after one of his unfortunate adventures. It's a smell you just can't mistake for anything else. He never had to tell us what happened. We smelled what happened.

Skunks are basically peace seeking . . . something my brother should have learned! It's said they only spray when they feel threatened. How Howie managed to threaten as many skunks as he did, or find himself at the rear end of the cute furry animal, we'll never know. (1)

~

It was a beautiful, dry fall day. I was walking home from school one afternoon with my best friend. We were having the usual girl talk about boys we thought were cute, or songs we liked, or who wore what that day, or what to do on the weekend, at least after chores were done.

Suddenly, I heard my mother's voice emanating loudly from the family farmhouse. I hadn't even turned into the path to the house yet, but I had a sneaking suspicion that Howie had caused this commotion—again.

"Not again, Howard!" she cried. "Of all the creatures there are, why must it always be a skunk?"

"It was just walking across the road, Mom, and got scared when it saw me," Howie said.

"Then just quietly walk away, son!" she said. "Now, don't move! Just stand there. Don't you dare come into the house!"

"I only wanted to see where it was going," said Howie.

Mom turned and scurried back into the house, leaving the back screen door open, and continued yelling unhappy phrases out to Howie. Then, the drill began, as she made trips back and forth into the pantry and out again carrying huge steel buckets of pure tomato juice. Howie rolled his eyes.

"Stand still and cover your eyes," she instructed, hoisting up a heavy pail of the red, pungent juice over Howie's head and showering him—clothes and all—with a good dousing.

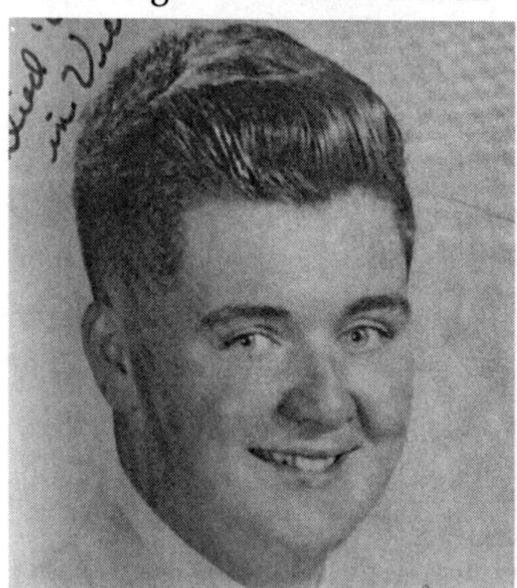

Howard L. Bowen, or "Howie" as he was known by his family and friends, is described by one of his sisters as, "fun loving, always happy".

"Yeow, Mom!" blubbered my brother.

"One more time, Howie," Mom said.

Howie just stood in the back yard, dripping tomato juice from head to toe, grateful that the juice smell seemed to be winning over skunk aroma. Mom reappeared with a second, sloshing bucket and christened my brother once again with the eradicating liquid.

"Now, run as fast as you can into the tub and turn on

the shower full blast! Let it run all over you and your clothes then take them off. Just leave 'em in the tub. I'll have to clean it all up, later, anyway. Soap up real good—all over—a couple of times then dry off," she said. "And don't forget to scrub that hair!"

And, so it was about every four weeks or so, until winter set in and the skunk population had a breather!

Farming: An American Symbol

"The one image I have of Howard is him sitting on Dad's red International tractor. Howie wrote in his high school yearbook that when he graduated, he wanted to be a farmer like Dad and Granddad. "

~ *Janet (Bowen) Dennis, sister*

The farmer's life is as American as it gets. It is a singular way of life, involving exceptionally hard work, long hours and complete family involvement based on family tradition, usually.

Our paternal grandfather, Jess Bowen, Sr. (1883-1949), was a successful farmer in Clarendon. He was married to our grandmother, Radie Dolan (1887-1971). They had 15 grandchildren and 26 great-grandchildren. Our father, Burton Bowen (1907-1994), was a dairy farmer. Our mother, Mary Dunn Bowen, was the traditional farming housewife.

Like most farm families, we didn't have a lot of extra money, but we were pretty self-sufficient. We raised pigs, ducks, chickens, turkeys and rabbits. Each winter, we traded a pig for a quarter of beef from another farmer. Mom canned everything we grew, including vegetables, fruit and even meat. She even baked her own bread. It smelled so delicious baking in the oven.

Dad was also an avid hunter, so we often had wild game (rabbit, pheasant and deer) at our table. Dad hunted with his dog. I think he was named Smoky or Red. In any event, I felt sorry for him when he was tied up outside. So, I brought him water and some leftovers and just talked to him. One time, I even crawled into his dog house with him to keep him company. (That was before I knew I should be afraid of spiders and fleas!)

Our house was always clean and orderly and there was always plenty to eat. We did our chores, before and after school, like feeding and milking the cows, pitching hay, cleaning the barns or making repairs to the house. It didn't always feel like work and we often had fun doing it!

We would ride the grain elevator up to the top floor of the barn and goof off a little with a break. When our chores were done, we did what kids do; often playing baseball alongside the house.

As kids, we never felt short-changed. We were a happy, proud bunch! Those were good times.

A-Butchering We Will Go

Every late fall or early winter, neighbors would regularly plan a butchering day at one of the area farms. This was a big to-do, with lots of planning and heavy work.

Large kettles of water were heated to boiling atop a red hot wood fire for scalding pigs, or sometimes a calf or sheep. Large hooks were secured above barn doors and onto trees to hang up the slaughtered animals. I remember that four families usually participated; each family helping each other.

My mother always cooked slabs of fat from the pigs in the oven of our cook stove. She poured off the grease into cans and stored them in the pantry or basement, where it was cool. This supplied her with cooking lard for pie crusts and frying. Just about everything that was produced on a farm was either prepared for meals or saved and used somehow. It was very economical and the quality of products was quite good. (2)

Boys Will Be Boys

No opportunity was ever missed by young farm boys to taunt and scare girls! Some things never change. The day after a butchering took place, some of the boys would retrieve a pig

The Bowen family working the family farm. Howie wrote in his year book that he wanted to be a farmer like his dad and grand dad.

bladder—or tail—or foot—or even an eye—and show them to screaming girls at school. Boys will be boys!

Howie was a little too young to participate in this gory game. But, I'm sure he would have been one of the ring leaders if he were older!

A Community Grieves

"I was nine when you were killed and I remember everything that day from the time I got off the school bus. Although everyone told me you were killed, even after your funeral and seeing you in the casket, I was SURE you'd be back. I waited and waited for you. I know you, Mom and Dad are looking over the four of us and I want you to know I love and still miss you."

~ *Debbie Bowen-Roe, sister*

"Everybody knew everybody in town. We went to all the funerals. It was really rough. We were a close knit family," says Janet Bowen Dennis.

Jane Bowen Robinson remembers her brother, Howard, as "the life of the party".

"He was happy-go-lucky and good natured. He was involved in school basketball and always had good grades," she recalls.

The Battle of Ap Cha Do

At the time of the battle of Ap Cha Do on November 8, 1966, the First Battalion was part of Operation Attleboro. I was soon to find myself in a stretch of dense jungle in Vietnam surrounded by VC and NVA and taking heavy fire.

The days leading up to the battle the First Battalion was stationed at Phuoc Vinh. The city was considered something of a safe zone with the North Vietnamese stronghold being more than ten miles to the north. The only way into the city from that direction was an unpaved narrow road covered in crushed red rock. Stationed along with us were additional Special Forces and three batteries of artillery. We considered the entire area well-guarded and defended.

I didn't know it at the time, but days before we were called into battle, American forces positioned just north of us had come under heavy assault. Since mid-October, they had occupied a base camp just south of a key village to the west and a plantation to the east. On November 3rd, they began to take sniper fire from the cover of thick jungle.

The morning of November 4th, Major General William E. Depuy, commander of the Big Red One—went up in a helicopter to survey the situation. While flying over heavily occupied enemy territory, he saw our reconnaissance company, under intense enemy fire. Some of that enemy fire was then turned on his copter. Depuy returned to base where he immediately called for an all-out assault on the enemy position. Our battalion was called into the fight, and I was on my way.

Depuy's strategy was to send us behind enemy lines so we could hit the Viet Cong from the north while his men did so from the south. On the 5th of November, we were taken from Phuoc Vinh by C-123 aircraft to just south of the plantation. The next morning, at 1035 hours, we were airlifted by helicopters to Landing Zone Two, an area of jungle to the north which had been cleared of the enemy by another group from our battalion.

No sooner had our transport helicopters cleared the treetops on takeoff, we took on enemy fire from the Viet Cong hiding beneath the thick cover of the jungle just to the north. One of the copters went down in fire and smoke, killing all but two of the occupants.

Despite these initial losses, it looked like it was going to be a basic operation. It took us less than an hour to secure the Landing Zone and surrounding ground. For most of the day to follow, all was relatively quiet. At approximately 5:45 in the evening, a platoon of ours out doing reconnaissance chanced upon some VC, killing three of them. There was no further contact that day.

The next morning, we moved south, sweeping the area of the previous day's fighting. There was no additional contact with the enemy. That night we established a perimeter and settled in, the second part of our battalion nearby. We had been ordered to continue south the next day before returning to base.

The NVA had other plans.

On the night of November 7, we again set up a defensive position and secured our perimeter. We were concerned about a network of VC trails found crisscrossing the dense jungle. Such trails often meant a large enemy presence. We kept watch throughout the night but had no enemy contact.

That next morning, Lieutenant Colonel Jack C. Whitted, out of Panama City, Florida, informed command that we would be conducting reconnaissance by fire. For those not familiar, it is a tactic in which large amounts of gunfire are discharged randomly into the jungle with the objective of tricking the enemy into revealing its position. We concentrated mortar fire to the north.

Shortly after the mortar fire started at 6:00 in the morning, two trip flares were set off upon our northern perimeter indicating an enemy presence. We started to receive small arms and automatic weapon fire upon our position. We had Claymore mines just outside our perimeter. Some of these had been discovered by the VC and disarmed, but most went off as planned, keeping the enemy from overtaking our lines.

Our second battalion nearby, believed the activity they were hearing was part of our Reconnaissance by Fire. They ignored it and continued with their morning routine of shaving and cleaning their weapons.

By 6:20 a.m., we had begun to take on heavy fire from automatic weapons. An all-out frontal attack soon followed. We managed to hold it off primarily due to our Claymores. We also requested and received air and artillery support. After about fifteen minutes of intense contact, the NVA was forced to fall back.

The enemy mounted a second attack a little more than ten minutes later, concentrating their efforts on our position once again. We again held them off with the Claymores and the aid of air and artillery. The VC quickly withdrew, but continued to fire at us with small arms and automatics, and to throw grenades. This indicated just how close to us they were.

No more than five minutes later, the VC and NVA attacked a third time. Intent on penetrating our perimeter to the west, they launched attacks every five minutes, sending wave after wave of infantry. Supported by air and artillery, which rained thousands of shells down upon the surrounding jungle, they again were forced to retreat.

Despite the pounding they were taking, the VC had managed to establish a position with a machinegun, and were directly firing upon our perimeter. Our casualties were mounting. Seeing my opportunity, I crawled out from my position. Staying as low to the ground as I could, I went about fifty feet to get myself parallel to where the machinegun was positioned. Taking aim on the enemy gunner, I blasted away with my 12-guage shotgun. I caught him with the first shot.

The machinegun no longer posed a threat, but with automatic

weapons fire pouring out of the trees, I made my way from position to position resupplying my men with any ammunition and hand grenades I could get my hands on. Smoke heavy in the air and visibility reduced to just a few feet, a member of our unit, Howard Bowen, took a hit and went down. But I couldn't get to him.

Only minutes later, a helicopter landed in a nearby clearing, taking automatic weapon fire the whole time. Among those who disembarked was Father Mike Quealy from New York City. Despite bullets flying all around, he began to administer last rites to the dead and dying. While helping to evacuate some of the wounded to the waiting helicopters, he was caught in crossfire and killed. He would go on to receive the Congressional Medal of Honor for these actions.

By 8:30, our contact with the enemy had been reduced to small arms fire, much of which was thwarted by helicopter gunships. Less than an hour and a half later, our patrols were sent to the outer perimeter to search for additional Viet Cong. We encountered some snipers, but these were easily handled. By 11:00 a.m., the battle was over.

With the remaining VC and NVA having fled, Colonel Pendleton and his men swept the area. They discovered an extensive enemy base in the jungle which occupied an area more than a mile long. The combined VC and NVA forces had been fiercely protecting what had been at the time the largest ammunition stores ever captured by US Forces. Included were 19,000 grenades, a Claymore factory, more than a half-ton of explosives, and 400 Bangalore torpedoes. The base had been carefully concealed from overhead by tying the treetops together and building underground bunkers.

Ultimately, the battle of Ap Cha Do resulted in 399 VC and NVA casualties. Our side suffered 21 killed and 42 wounded. Later I learned that Howard Bowen was among the dead.

Kirk J. James, SP 4, 25th Infantry Division, 1st Battalion

Howard Bowen died at the battle of Ap Cha Do by small arms fire on November 8, 1966. His family was devastated.

"Howard – I remember when you worked at General Electric with me. You were such a good person. I visited your grave the other day. I brought some flowers. I miss you, Howard."

~ Rick Clark, co-worker

Like young George Fischer and many of his other friends, Howie loved fast cars and racing at the Lancaster Speedway. He was hard to miss in his 1956 turquoise Chevy convertible, among other models in his car collection.

But, it was his last car – a white 1961 Chevy Impala – that was most memorable. My father, however, couldn't bear the thought of selling the car locally after my brother's death, and having to see someone else driving it down the road and around town. So he decided to sell it to an out-of-state used car dealer in Pennsylvania. My father said, "That car needed to be anywhere but Holley."

~ Janet (Bowen) Dennis, sister

CHAPTER TEN

The Tet Offensive

DURING THE TIME OF THE WAR IN VIETNAM, Walter Cronkite was arguably the most respected voice in media, and perhaps even in the country as a whole. On February 27, 1968, Cronkite appeared on national television and told the nation that the war in Vietnam was—despite a gallant and heroic effort on the part of the United States—unwinnable. He called the war, at best, a stalemate. The only alternative, according to Cronkite, was a "terrible escalation…for [which]…the enemy can match us… [And] with each escalation, the world comes closer to the brink of cosmic disaster." (1)

Cronkite's address to the nation came a month or so after the beginning of the Tet Offensive—named for the Vietnamese New Year, a country-wide military strike by the North Vietnamese against the ARVN and US troops. The offensive took place during the Christmas holiday—much of Vietnam was devoutly Catholic, and a time when military activity by mutual truce between Hanoi and Saigon had been traditionally suspended.

In late January, the North Vietnamese Army and thousands of guerrilla irregulars simultaneously moved against the American firebase at Khe Sanh and a host of major cities throughout the South. The objective of the plan, designed by General Giap, was to divide the American forces, obligating them to respond to the hundreds of city-based attacks while leaving less of a force to defend the base. Giap believed that the fall of the base, much like the French debacle at Dien Bien Phu would reverse the North's worsening position, leaving the United States demoralized and willing to negotiate an end to the conflict.

Prior to the attack on Khe Sanh, the North Vietnamese, for months, had been smuggling both arms and guerrilla fighters into the key cities and larger towns of the South. The arms were brought in using whatever means possible, including hidden in food deliveries, taxicabs, and coffins. The guerrillas, primarily NVA irregulars, entered in small groups of two and three, often masquerading as peasants, regular everyday city folk, and ARVN soldiers on holiday. Many of these guerrillas were housed by sympathizers, especially in the poorer quarters where the citizens were less likely to support the government.

At the same time these measures were being taken in the cities, General Giap had amassed multiple battalions of forces around the hills and roads surrounding and leading into Khe Sanh. Khe Sanh had been a stronghold of the French prior to their defeat at Dien Bien Phu.

Noting the build-up of Viet Cong around Khe Sanh, Commander Westmoreland ordered the firebase reinforced, sending in an additional 6,000 troops. Estimates counted no less than 20,000 VC, and perhaps as many as 40,000 in the surrounding hills.

On January 31, 1968, the first day of the Vietnamese New Year, the guerrilla attacks by the North Vietnamese commenced in the major cities and towns, more than 100 all told. These were not mass attacks by whole battalions, but specific attacks undertaken by small groups and aimed at key city structures, such as police stations, radio stations, government offices, local garrisons, and military headquarters.

The American Embassy in Saigon was one of these targets. Nineteen fighters from the National Liberation Front, riding in taxis, easily over-powered the five MPs at the gate, killing two, and passed within the walls. However, their efforts to breach the embassy itself—including the use of anti-tank rockets—were repelled by the Marines inside and reinforcements which arrived by helicopter. When the fighting was over, all nineteen guerrillas lay dead in the courtyard.

Elsewhere in Saigon, fourteen NLF fighters forced their way into a radio station. There they withstood a siege by South Vietnamese forces for nearly a day before blowing up the building and themselves with it.

The Tet Offensive, although described as a military victory for the U.S. and South Vietnamese Army, was the catalyst for the media and political leadership of the country, to question for the first time, the ability of America to win the war.

Throughout the city, the North Vietnamese irregulars entrenched themselves mostly in the poorer quarters, rushing out to engage the South Vietnamese troops in hand-to-hand combat, killing and wounding as many as possible, and then fading back into the shanties and alleys, only to strike again elsewhere. (2)

It was the same scene in all 100 cities.

This type of guerrilla and hand-to-hand fighting went on for more than six weeks. With no other option, the South Vietnamese and the Americans resorted to shelling the guerrilla strongholds from above, reducing block upon city block of buildings and structures to rubble. By the middle of February, most of the insurgents had been killed or routed.

The Battle for Hue

One of the cities hit the hardest was Hue, the sacred home of Viet Nam's largest Buddhist population and the site of the killings ordered by Ngo Dinh Diem, the President in 1963.

At the start of the offensive, and primarily due to the support of the city's residents and 10 NVA battalions, the insurgents quickly seized control of Hue. Only the ARVN headquarters and the US garrison stood strong. Finally, on February 25, following intense bombing by US fighter jets, the city was taken back. Nevertheless, in scenes reminiscent of Stanley Kubrick's Full Metal Jacket, which was set in Hue, snipers continued to take lives from the bombed out sections of the city. Just in Hue alone over 100 American soldiers lost their lives, and almost 400 ARVN. The losses to the NVA and the insurgents was more than fifteen times those numbers.

Meanwhile, the siege on Khe Shan began for real on January 21. Thousands of NVA surged out of the jungle intent on crossing the river running alongside the airbase and breaking through American lines. The attack was thwarted by intense firepower, but shortly after, the entirety of the runway was blasted and put out of commission by enemy mortars.

Fierce fighting would continue unabated until the first week of April, during which time the American forces were pinned down, moving out from cover only to repel repetitive attacks on their lines and to retrieve supplies parachuted in by aircraft and helicopters passing overhead.

Finally, in that first week of April, and following intense bombing and the use of napalm on the enemy positions by B-52s and strike aircraft, including positions which were literally on the defensive perimeter, the siege was ended and the base was no longer in danger of being overrun.

While the Tet Offensive took the South Vietnamese and American forces by surprise, and had impressive success initially, the overall failure of the NLF and the NVA to gain the support of the general population was its undoing. A majority neither trusted the Saigon government nor the communists. Instead of taking up arms, as Ho Chi Minh had hoped, they remained neutral. The offensive defeated, and their identities exposed, the NLF and the irregulars were forced to flee into the jungle, thereby bringing collapse to the networks they had built up throughout the cities. (3)

When all was said and done, the Tet Offensive cost the North 45,000 lives to the 6,000 lost by the South and the United States combined. Nevertheless, Ho Chi Minh and General Giap accomplished what they set out to do. They showed they were willing to die for their cause, and that they would continue to do so for as long as necessary, taking as many South Vietnamese and American lives as possible. It was that attitude, and the means by which they demonstrated it, which eventually led Walter Cronkite, as voice of the people, and eventually Washington, to come to the realization that Viet Nam was a war that couldn't be won.

CHAPTER ELEVEN

Gary E. Bullock

September 18, 1942–January 31, 1967

January 18, 1967

Dear Mom,

I hope this letter will find you and the rest of the family in the very best of health. I am doing ok even though I am going crazy about coming home for good.

I got your letter today and I was very pleased to hear from you and all. I am sorry that I wasn't home for Aunt Jane's funeral. I feel bad because every time somebody dies in our family I have been in another country. I am glad that everybody else is ok. How did your mother take Aunt Jane's death?

Well I can get up to $100 a month from the government for going to school for 3 years after I get out of the army.

There isn't too much more I can say except that I love you all and I want to come home. So, I will close for now.

God bless.

Love always,

Gary

Going Door to Door

Some people say that good products can sell themselves no matter what it is or who's selling them. In my grandfather's case, it's quite possible that people bought whatever my grandfather, Jay Bullock, was selling because he was so likeable and engaging. Besides, a good word about a product from a man whose family members were hard working farmers themselves, just like his customers, couldn't hurt.

Grandpa was a door-to-door Watkins Products salesman, representing a trusted, one-of-a-kind company that manufactured and sold an eclectic variety of household cleaning aids and holistic health products long before they were trendy. Watkins' products had an excellent reputation. They still do. But, the combination of Grandpa's once-a-month visits and some much needed liniment had to brighten one's day and literally ease the pain.

Gary Bullock's grandfather, Jay Bullock, is shown standing next to his Watkins Products truck. Bullock's first territory was known as the "Black North", so named because at one time trees were so dense in that area sun light was not able to penetrate to the ground.

Company owner, Joseph Ray (J.R.) Watkins, of Plainview, Minnesota, developed his own formula at home for aching, tired muscles. The all-natural liniment he discovered to relieve pain contained camphor from evergreen trees and capsicum from red peppers. The success of the product (first manufactured for sale across the country around 1868) was astounding. At last, people who performed physically strenuous jobs, worked their own land, or who suffered from maladies associated with muscle and body aches, found relief from Watkins' simple but potent liniment. (1)

~

There was a time when I voluntarily visited with people in our area, mostly elders, who would be considered shut-ins, today. They rarely ventured forth into the world, except on rare occasion. Age, illness or weariness kept them close to home. I was able and willing to travel just to be company for some of them. Our time together always taught me something; not something you'd learn in a classroom, but something important to your own life. I wasn't employed to do this; I did it because I thought it was the right thing to do. It was the way we were raised. When you reach out to others amazing things happen; many of them, unexpected.

One day I went to Hamlin, one of the towns on my grandfather's original route in his "territory", the Black North. People usually don't go to this place as a destination. You have to want to go there, because it's so remote. Hamlin was a town situated north of Holley in an area aptly named because the forest growth was so dense, that light couldn't penetrate it. The area was also comprised largely of stagnant swamp land; which invited the

A rare 1914 photo showing the Bullock clan celebrating the birthday of Gary's maternal grandmother in Kuckville, New York.

spread of the dreaded disease, malaria. Yet, families managed to live and produce and raise families there.

In the early 1900s, my grandfather regularly traveled the Ridge Road, a Native American walking trail, originally, through these areas. Later, "the Ridge" became one of the prominent paths for the first settlers of the area. (2)

~

Minnie Klafehn, an engaging 85-year-old, invited me into her home and offered me a cup of delicious herb tea and homemade lavender scones. The smell of them alone, with small pats of butter melting in their rocky crevices, made me relax in a different, refreshing kind of way.

I felt as if I was spending time in a previous, quieter life. Our conversation, however, burned bright for another reason. Minnie told me that she compared my visit to that of the Watkins man who used to deliver products to her family when she was a child. His visit, she recounted, was a happy thing. They never knew for sure when he and his horse drawn carriage would come lumbering up the dirt road to the house; but when that day came, it was cause for celebration, good will, and smiles!

~

"Momma! Momma, he's coming!" sang little Minnie. The eight-year-old's fair, blond pigtails bounced evenly as she skipped up to the front door and continued her announcement inside the house.

"C'mon, Momma! It's Mr. Bullock!" echoed her older brother, Karl, who looked up distractedly from his task of unearthing whatever might have been living beneath some choice rocks. At 10, he was of course, the "grown-up" on the scene until his mother came outside. Until then, he had to size up the situation rather seriously.

Karl dropped the worn plastic shovel, stood up and walked to the front fence of the property. He shifted his weight to one leg, while he bent the other knee in preparation for Mr. Bullock's arrival. He decided this was a good, casual pose that made him look like a man of the world. It didn't matter that he was barely able to see over the top of the fence and the rusty knots of steel that bordered it like an ancient trim. He couldn't see the wagon yet, but he recognized the familiar clip pity-clop of a horse's hooves. So, he waited . . . almost patiently.

~

Grandpa always said that his horse seemed to already know which way to draw the carriage. How in the world could he have made these deliveries without her, he wondered. She knew how to sidestep annoying brambles on the old dirt road and hold steady on the slippery patches of sickly, sticky blackberries underfoot. Grandpa always said she was a loyal traveling companion with a sweet nature.

As Minnie recalled, the sun was trying its best to shine on a mild fall afternoon as the sturdy wagon lumbered up the path to the lone, wooden-frame house. Grandpa didn't mind the ride through this area at all, because he knew that he'd encounter little or absolutely no competition at all from other vendors or get caught up in the business of others because of the precarious location. Its unfortunate geographic facts made his travel to homes in this less than desirable location, even more necessary and readily welcomed.

~

As the path wound a bit closer to the house, Grandpa characteristically felt in his pocket for the children's "surprises". Just as he would be sure to carry extra sugar cubes for his horse

Clara, he also came bearing sweet treats or small, inexpensive toys for his customers' children. He always brought something for them. Sometimes it would be little dainty sandwich crackers; sometimes jelly beans; sometimes a tiny tin airplane, or camel, or elephant. That day it was crystal clear rock candy on a string. Nothing but hard sugar water, but the smiles on the children's faces would make him as happy as they were when they popped the little craggy shaped chunks into their mouths.

To my extreme delight, it became clear to both Minnie and me that she was the little girl who, along with her older brother, announced and anxiously anticipated the Watkins' Product salesman, my grandfather, Mr. Jay Bullock.

A Universal Language

When people raise their voices in song, a special kind of communication happens, even if you don't know the song or the people involved. There's just something joyous and unselfish about bringing the gift of music and song to anyone who decides to listen and participate.

I'm told my grandfather was a wonderful singer and sang for many years in a barber shop choir with his four brothers and his father, our great grandfather. It's one thing to be entertained by a small, talented, all male signing group; but it's exceptional when they are all related to each other. I imagine they had a lot of fun doing this together.

(I wouldn't be surprised if Grandpa sang as he traveled along his sales route!)

In God We Trust
The First Methodist Church of Holley

Socially, the offering of music and song can also be seen as a spiritual bonding experience. The Bullocks were certainly social people and church going was important to them. In this effort, my grandmother joined my grandfather in stepping up their participation in The First Methodist Church of Holley.

In her comprehensive pamphlet, "The History of the First Methodist Church, Holley, New York (1869-1966)", Miss Irene M. Gibson, a lifelong Holley resident, wrote, "Always from the start, the church was blessed by an excellent choir. The singers numbered about twenty. Every Sunday night the church is said to have been crowded to hear the splendid music and to listen to the ministers, who were excellent preachers."

Founding the Methodist Episcopal Church

In May of 1869, a meeting of future congregants and interested parties came together to found and organize the Methodist Episcopal Church of Holley. Their intention was to build a church from the ground up. Some were so resolved in this mission that they pledged a total of approximately $3,200 at the outset of the project.

By July of the same year, a site for the church was purchased from Hiram Frisbee, one of Holley's founding fathers. The land was conveniently located at the north end of the Public Square. Soon, a fine brick building emerged and the cornerstone was laid. Nine months later, the First Methodist Episcopal Church was born and was dedicated on April 27, 1870.

On the Sunday following the dedication, a Sunday school was promptly organized. It soon served an average of 120 "scholars in attendance".

When the physical construction of the church was completed, the total cost of all was $12,000. On the day of its dedication, an unpaid balance of $7,000 remained. The entire amount was quickly absorbed in community "subscriptions"* or scheduled payments. (3)

Typically, Holley

The kind of moral perseverance and deep social commitment to a cause on the part of Holley's residents was especially evident in their steadfast resolve to found and physically construct its First Methodist Episcopal Church, from the ground up.

Holley's people saw a need and answered it; contributed to it, embraced it as their own, and shared its programs and benefits with others in the community. It was a divine labor of love and fulfillment.

Living—and giving—in this way would continue as examples of the indefatigable strength of character of Holley's populace.

The First Methodist Episcopal Church still proudly faces Holley's town square. It is officially listed on the United States National Register of Historic Places as is the town of Holley, as a United States Historic District.

The Church as a Homestead

The church, back then, was the primary vehicle for social events. My grandfather served on the Board of Trustees from 1942-1945. My grandmother was Vice-President of the Women's Foreign Missionary Service, tasked with the goal of elevating and "christening" their sisters in far flung "heathen" lands, such as China, Japan and Korea. This was a cause she supported for many years. (4)

Our Parents

"My father, Dayton C. Bullock (1901-1999), was a gentle soul. He was a member of the church for over 20 years and served on its Board of Trustees. When the church merged with the Disciples United Methodist Church in Holley, he continued his avid and supportive participation. My father involved himself in church repairs—wire brush and painting the basement block walls—while my mother served on the Landscape Committee.

Gary's mother and father are shown during choir practice. They were both prominent members of Holley's Methodist Church. Gary's mother is shown dressed in white and his father is standing to her left.

"He sang in the church choir, offering his pure tenor voice. He was also a Mary Jane Candies salesman when he wasn't working on the local railroad . . . or helping my grandfather complete his Watkins route when he was too ill to do it alone.

"My father was a soft-hearted man who did not hunt because he simply didn't want to kill anything! One of my mother's favorite sayings, "It's hot enough to boil an owl," was never really understood and we never dared to ask! Actually boiling an owl or any living thing, for that matter, would not have sat well with my father.

"Both of my parents were well-read and interested in current issues, regularly reading Reader's Digest, Reader's Digest Books, US News & World Report, and a variety of local newspapers and newsletters. For my mother, the reference to "boiling an owl", may have come from New England (Maine or New Hampshire) printed sources that either coined or repeated the saying. In any case, it did stop us in our tracks as we imagined what might have befallen an innocent owl in high temperatures."

Sharon (Bullock) Root, Sister

Team 99

During the Vietnam War, the United States armed forces relied heavily on the efforts of a then covert unit of soldiers known as MACV-SOG: Military Assistance Command, Vietnam-Studies and Observation Group. The unit consisted of soldiers with a special mission—get in behind enemy lines to harass and divert the enemy. Working in small groups, the MACV units lived among the South Vietnamese soldiers, removed and isolated from their own battalions, and relying on trust to covertly engage the enemy behind enemy lines, and then get out again alive. (5)

Gary pictured in High School year book. He is described by his sister as a "prankster", who loved basketball, and was "popular with the girls".

Recalling his perception of the ARVN soldiers he interacted with on a daily basis, John S., with the 99 MACV at Ky Vinh, a fish net factory, says of the Bict Dong Quan—South Vietnamese soldiers—"I found them to be good soldiers and was proud to have served with them. I had many ARVN friends, as I was the only enlisted man [among them]. I often wonder how they are doing; if they are still alive." (Team 99 Duc Hoa, 2016).

John M., a MACV member with another team, relates a story revealing the importance of camaraderie and trust among the team and the ARVN.

"It was in November of '68," he recalls, "Thanksgiving Day, to be exact. Bubba, one of my fellow MACV team members, and I were enjoying the meal with all the trimmings. Just then, we get the call to go out. VC in numbers had been located just the other side of the Cambodian border. Our mission was to find out where. We were to be joined by Sau, an ARVN. There was also an interpreter named Heip.

"We were dropped into the landing zone by helicopter. The landscape here was thin, not very different from the wooded areas in New Jersey where I used to squirrel hunt as a boy. Once on the ground, the first thing we did was lay a line of claymores, just in case we ran into trouble on the way back out.

"Moving forward, we spotted a thin line of smoke swirling up over the trees. We were certain it was VC. As we neared, we realized we were right in the middle of a VC camp recently abandoned. Sau had become visibly nervous and was talking real fast to Heip. Despite his obvious trepidation and his uncanny intuition when it came to the VC, I moved us further into the wood. I was hoping to find a weapons cache or some other evidence of their presence, maybe tell us how many.

"Suddenly, Sau's eyes got as big as saucers. He's pointing into the trees ahead of us. Then I saw it, too—the tops of the helmets of VC, and they're coming right at us. I grabbed my radio and tell the copter to get back here and pick us up, and while they're at it, bring along the gunships. We turned and made a run for the landing zone.

"No sooner did we get going, Sau spotted NVA coming at us from our flank. We placed another claymore between us and them and got going. We barely made it to the cover of the trees, when the wire got tripped and the claymore exploded. We caught up to Bubba and the others, who had also set up a line of claymores of their own. It was our only hope to delay them long enough to make it to the landing zone.

"We made it only a few yards further when we realized we weren't going to make it if we didn't do something to slow them down. Together we stopped and turned, pointed our weapons and started firing. Bubba and I had M79s. The ARVN had automatic CR-15s. We saw the helmets drop as the enemy took cover.

"We had our chance. We made a dash for the helicopter which

had just landed. We jumped aboard, and just as the copter started to lift, the NVA came through the trees. The one out front lifted his weapon to fire, and I sent off a burst of rounds. They caught him in the chest, and I watched as his feet and head kept moving forward, but the rest of him was driven back by the blast, folding him in half and dropping him to the ground.

"The last we saw of the VC and NVA they were moving towards that first line of claymores we had put down. But by then the copter was getting us up and over the trees. Safely back at base, Bubba and I returned to our Thanksgiving Dinner, and our ARVN friends were off to a meal of their own."

While the individual stories of so many members of this covert and dedicated unit are similar to those of these two soldiers, the MACV-SOG was disbanded in the early 1970s. Some suggest it was due to a change in military tactics on both sides, but primarily the willingness of the VC and NVA to engage in open combat, thereby minimizing the role of the MACV-SOG. Others point out that the unit simply was becoming less effective due to an unwillingness to adapt. Finally, others point to the actual dynamics itself, suggesting that the side-by-side interaction with and trust of the ARVN made it too easy for the VC and NVA to infiltrate MACV

Gary photographed while serving with MACV, Team 99 in Vietnam. He was awarded the Bronze Star for his service.

operations with agents of their own posing as South Vietnamese, thereby rendering the MACV ineffective. Regardless, the heroic deeds of these special soldiers will live on in the stories of those who made it home. One of our own team members who did not make it back home was Gary E. Bullock from Holley, New York. He died on January 31, 1967 from incoming mortar fire. For his service in Vietnam he received the Bronze Star posthumously.

Fred Ramsey, MACV Team 99...

Gary

Gary was easygoing, happy-go-lucky and was a devoted member of our church. He made it a point to see Billy Graham when he came to Syracuse.

He liked to play basketball (he was the tallest in his class), was good looking and had many girlfriends. My mother received Gary's last letter from Vietnam just four days before we were notified of his death. We were devastated. You could never recover from it because of all the other Holley boys that were killed in Vietnam.

The whole town turned out for each funeral.

Sharon (Bullock) Root, Sister

CHAPTER TWELVE

My Lai Massacre

THERE IS A SCENE IN OLIVER STONE'S **1986** MOVIE depiction of the Vietnam War, *Platoon,* in which the star, Charlie Sheen, comes to the aid of a young South Vietnamese girl who is about to be violated by the platoon members alongside of whom he is fighting. Sheen's character, Chris Taylor, is collectively slurred by those soldiers, whose references to the girl reduce her to something less than human. This scene, down to the murder of villagers and the burning of the village, is a portrait representative of the events of the My Lai Massacre. (1)

Following the Tet Offensive, the NVA and the VC, began to resort more significantly to guerrilla tactics, striking when and where they could, and then immediately melting into the general population, hiding their weapons and donning the clothes of farmers and villagers.

Frustrated by the lack of conventional military style engagements, U.S. forces adopted new tactics of their own. The My Lai Massacre was an illustration of those tactics taken to an extreme.

Charlie Company was an especially close group of young men. They had trained together in the States prior to heading to Vietnam, including special jungle warfare training in Hawaii.

In Vietnam, Charlie Company was deployed to the province of

Quang Ngai in the heart of the country. The province was given the nickname *Pinkville* by the soldiers, an intentionally derogatory term identifying the local Vietnamese as *meat*.

On a daily basis, the platoon would go out into the thick jungle to find and engage the VC units in what were called search and destroy missions. However, the VC rarely showed themselves, using the cover of the trees and hills to conceal snipers, mines, and booby traps. Charlie Company members were routinely maimed, dismembered, or killed.

With frustration mounting, on March 15, the platoon commanders learned from faulty intelligence that a large contingency of Viet Cong soldiers were positioned in the village of My Lai, population 700. The platoon was alerted that it would finally have the opportunity to fight an enemy it could see.

On the morning of March 16, Captain Medina told his men that everyone in the village would be a VC soldier or a VC sympathizer. There would be no innocents. Capitalizing on the platoon's intense emotions and eagerness to engage, Lieutenant William Calley ordered his men to enter the village firing, to shoot and kill anyone on sight. They did exactly that.

Once the smoke had cleared following the first assault, villagers began to emerge from their homes, wide-eyed and shaken. For a moment there was nothing but silence. Without explanation, and despite the presence of nothing more than old folks, women, and children, the soldiers again opened fire. When all was said and done, more than 300 peasants and farmers lay dead, 50 of them three years of age or younger, and none of them Viet Cong. Later, the platoon was to discover that the VC were actually all the way on the other side of the province.

For almost a year and a half, news of the events at My Lai were kept from the American people. However, disturbed by the events, a soldier from Charlie Company, Ron Ridenhour, sent letters to various officials in Washington. Though Ridenhour himself was not present at My Lai, he recommended an investigation of what he called "something rather dark and bloody." His letters went ignored. Ridenhour then brought his story to a reporter by the name of Seymour Hersh. The story of the massacre at My Lai then appeared in 30 newspapers and magazines, including *Newsweek, The Times,* and *The Cleveland Plain Dealer. The Cleveland Plain Dealer* published never before seen photos of the actual scene itself.

In addition, tales surfaced of actual My Lai incidents. Defenseless old men were run through with bayonets. Women and children down on their knees and praying—many Vietnamese were devout Catholics—were shot in the back of the head. One girl was raped and then killed. As for Calley, he was reported to have rounded up a group of villagers, ordered them into a ditch, and then he himself shot them all to death with an automatic weapon. There were other stories of mutilations, including soldiers who carved the letter 'C' into the chest of their victims, or who cut off fingers, hands, and scalps. At one point, a soldier, Robert Maples, refused Calley's order to shoot defenseless villagers, and in turn had Calley turn his weapon on him instead. There were also reports of a helicopter pilot who threatened to turn his guns on platoon soldiers to keep them from slaughtering an innocent family. (2)

In September of 1969, two months prior to the release of Hersh's story—an obvious indication of Washington's attempt at a cover-up, Lieutenant Calley was charged by the military with premeditated murder and sentenced to life in prison. Anti-war sentiment ran high at this time, and Washington was overwhelmed with support for Calley, who was seen as a scapegoat for all that was wrong with America's involvement in Viet Nam. President Nixon responded by releasing Calley. He served only four and a half months. Captain Medina was later acquitted, as well as all the other platoon members initially charged. (3)

The Massacre at My Lai remains a stain on the honor of the military of the United States, and a reminder to the world that atrocities of war are everlasting.

CHAPTER THIRTEEN

Gary L. Stymus

November 10, 1941-May 25, 1967

"My grandparents, Henry and Ethel Stymus, were muck farmers. Their parcel of land was located between South Manning Road east, to the Upper Holley Road. This section also included the farms of James Gaylord, Rudy Brant, Pete Bowen, Irving Kennedy and Fred and Ray Bowen. Most people are not familiar with muck farming."

~ *Duane Stymus, Gary's Brother*

Ode to the Muck Farmer

You know the adage. "If life gives you lemons, make lemonade". Feel free to substitute anything you have too *much* of in the above example—as in too much *muck*; in which case, you become a muck farmer.

This is exactly what my grandparents and parents did.

Approximately 100-years-ago, the Oak Orchard and the Tonawanda Swamp were drained to create the Elba Mucklands, simply known to local residents as *The Muck*.

For years, the industrious people of Orleans County have lived with and know all about muck. They also know how to deal with it in a productive way to make it work *for* them, instead of literally sinking in the process.

What is *Muck*?

Muck is a gift from nature that keeps on giving as it has for thousands of years. Muck is a fine, loosely packed soil enriched by naturally decaying vegetation of trees or plant life hanging over muddy swampland or hovering near it. Like the delicate consistency of fibrous peat soil, muck feels like sawdust when it is dry. It is very dark brown soil which appears black when wet.

Muck is born when this mixture of dying vegetation is submerged in swamp water that cannot drain off. This vegetation uses up the oxygen in the water, thus arresting further decay, while preserving as much as 80% of the organic content in the soil. Because it is so rich in organic matter, muck contains a high concentration of plant nutrients, such as nitrogen and phosphorus, which promote high crop yields.

There is, of course, a literal down side to the organic benefits produced by muck land. A combination of wind erosion that blows away soil, the oxidation of organic matter and the necessary compaction of soil by farm machinery, can reduce muck depth by approximately one inch per year, resulting in a muck *subsidence*, which is the sinking of the level of land.

This condition is so prevalent in some areas, that ramps are installed to drive farm machinery from muck roads to the fields. Because muck lands were formerly swamplands, they are naturally low-lying and accumulate water from higher ground. This land must be continuously tilled and pumped to keep it dry and workable.

Muck land is also subject to destructive droughts, floods, early frosts, plant diseases, such as onion smut (a fungal disease of onion plants which can exist for years, if infected spores contaminate fresh onion seeds), and pest infiltration, all of which reduce crop yields.

Underground fires are also a dangerous occurrence for muck farmers, mostly because they cannot be seen, but they can be smelled; and dry muck becomes a problem for everyone.

Exceptionally high winds can blow muck in all directions,

sometimes miles away from its original site, while muck workers may be blinded by it and cannot see 10-feet in front of them.

Traveling, windswept particles of muck are also a problem for neighbors, especially on laundry day. Imagine hanging a load of freshly washed bed sheets and towels on your outside line to dry, only to find them covered in a fine film of sepia-colored muck! This happened to more people than you'd imagine, including my grandmother.

For the most part, Orleans County's hundred-year history of muck farming has been accomplished on a seasonal basis by local and migrant workers. In the 40s and 50s, young people (my dad included) looked at mucking not only as a way to earn some extra money, but also as a way of having some summer fun. They'd come to work with lunch bags and pails full of food to last the whole day, as they toiled in the hot sun and the heat reflected by the soil. Local kids would also work weekends and during spring planting and fall harvesting. My dad remembers doing this.

Other workers—boys randomly hired on street corners by muck managers—padded the working ranks. And, as such, they were very much noticed by local girls, who cried and begged their fathers to let them join the muck workers. By all indications they were love struck by the obvious newcomers. In fact, one could say they were *muck* stuck by the presence of those young, hard-working, male strangers.

> *"I can't remember being in the house except for eating and sleeping. There was too much to do outside."*
>
> ~ Duane Stymus

So, as children and grandchildren of muck farmers, we naturally learned at an early age how to run machinery and perform every necessary task for working muck land.

We learned how to drive tractors and trucks; how to fill baskets or crates on a potato or onion picker; how to stack crates together; how to weed multiple rows of plants at one time, and how to mix the right proportions of chemical mix with water to spray the crops.

We also became familiar with the varieties and precise names of the potatoes, carrots and onions we grew. My grandfather was particularly proud of his Katahdin potatoes, Chatenay Coreless carrots and Yellow Globe onions. The names sounded so grand! (1)

Muckland, or the "Muck" as it is called, results from swamp land that has been drained leaving extremely fertile black soil. This black dirt is ideal for root crops such as potatoes and onions.

Of course, in addition to working on the farm, our lives were pretty much the same as other kids. We would go to school, play sports, fish and hunt a bit, enjoy local teen dances, race cars as many local boys did, and do our share of drinking, too! In the 40s and 50s, this was our life.

Coopers, Hoopers and Bowling Pins

Everyone in my family knew how to make things; useful and strong things. My maternal grandfather (of the Keable family of Brockport) was a *cooper*. A cooper crafts wooden barrels, buckets, casks, tubs and the like, which are used to store both "dry" and "wet" items.

The work of a cooper contains traces of Old World artisanship. The "dry" or "slack" cooper made circular containers suitable for storing and shipping dry goods, such as cereals, tobacco, flour and gunpowder. The "wet" or "tight" cooper made barrel-like containers to hold liquids, specifically intended for long-term storage, such as beer. The "white" cooper manufactured washtubs, buckets, butter churns and containers that held water and other liquids, but did not provide for the shipping of the liquids. And, the "general" cooper was responsible for working on and repairing containers on cargo ships, while in transit.

A sturdy metal hoop topped off and bound together the arced wooden slats of the barrels. The individual who made the metal hoops was called a *hooper*. This position was originally filled by a man acting as an assistant to a cooper. Over time, many coopers made the hoops themselves, thus bridging the "cooper / hooper" categories. (2)

Strrrrrike!

My father didn't have to travel far from home to "knock 'em down" — bowling pins, that is. For years, Dad owned and operated Shepard's Mill, a saw mill, which sat right across the road from our house. Among other things, they made bowling pins.

The mill first belonged to my father's stepfather before it belonged to Dad and his business partner, John Henderson, Jr. from Holley. Mr. Henderson was a former school teacher, who taught science at Holley Central.

Timber from sugar maple trees (in North America) was particularly valuable for commercial purposes. Its cousin is the Sycamore maple, commonly found in Europe. Here, sugar maple wood, often referred to as "hard" or "rock" maple, was the preferred choice for the manufacture of bowling pins, and sometimes, used in the construction of the actual bowling lanes.

Bowling pins were constructed of blocks of rock maple/sugar maple wood loosely formed into the general shape of the bowling pin required, then more acutely shaped on a lathe. Pins were then coated with a plastic-type material, painted and covered with a glossy finish.

However, as precious maple became scarce, bowling pins were allowed to be made with industry approved synthetics. Experts say that falling pins *sound* different, depending on the material they contain—wood or plastic. (3)

Mills that manufactured the coveted maple bowling pin realized nice profits. My father's mill made pins for Brunswick Bowling, a leading name in bowling supplies, and for the AMF (American Machine and Foundry).

The AMF operated over 240 bowling centers in the United States, and was once one of the nation's largest recreational equipment companies. From the 1970s through the early 1980s, however, the company declined in its ability to efficiently manage corporate growth, rising technology and global competition. (4)

Dad's mill eventually produced wooden boxes for shipping and storing cabbage, potatoes, onions and apples. Sawdust, itself, was also a precious commodity and in demand. In later years, farmers used it in their barns for bedding cattle.

Gary Stymus pictured in grade school. Gary was from a large family of eight children. He is described by his sister as the "quite one" and a "gentle soul".

"Our Family is Very Close, Clannish."

~ *Mrs. Helen Stymus, Gary's mother*

This—and other comments from our family—appeared in articles in The *Democrat & Chronicle* newspaper on February 11, 1973, after Gary's death. I think what my mother really wanted to convey in her remarks was that we were a close-knit bunch. We were family—and that's all we needed to know. Both of my parents and we kids believed that kinship was an important bond in times of happiness and sorrow. We were always aware of what was going on in each other's lives and grew together in a united way.

"A freak accident."

That's what one doctor said when he talked to Mom about how Gary died. He believed that Gary should never have died from the wound he suffered, and had he received crucial immediate medical attention right after he was shot, he would have most likely survived.

Pictured is Gary's boot camp army photo. At the time he joined the army he was married with two daughters. The marriage did not work out.

The *Democrat & Chronicle* reported the details of Gary's demise, as related by Gary's buddy, Charles Morrow, who also informed my parents of the same.

Gary's unit, the 25th Army Infantry Division, was preparing to execute a strategic maneuver to "pull back". Their positions in hot, clammy foxholes in Vietnam's dense and foreboding jungle terrain and oppressively hot and humid climate were endangered at every turn. The heat in the jungles would often reach 120 degrees. Men were battle fatigued, edgy and morose, cramped and sweaty; their uniforms filthy, their hands and glistening faces smeared with grime and perspiration.

Yet, in this God forsaken place, a Roman Catholic chaplain had celebrated Mass. Gary was heading back to his foxhole and to his machine gun when the Vietcong suddenly attacked. Their surprise strikes were commonplace, but this one, on May 25, 1967, claimed the lives of 17 Americans in the unit, including Gary's.

Gary was shot in the left armpit, which would not necessarily be considered a fatal injury. Medics, many of whom were only in their teens, were unable to reach him. According to Charles Morrow, they, too, were "pinned down" in the skirmish. He told my parents the truth: my brother bled to death, but "peacefully". Gary's official report of death stated, "Gary L. Stymus, PFC, died of a gunshot wound received in hostile ground action."

My mother said she was very grateful that his body was sent back to us. Other families of those missing in action or taken as prisoners of war, were not as fortunate. Gary was laid to rest at Mt. Albion Cemetery in a veteran's plot.

A Mother's Perspective

My mother treasured Gary's letters. In many of them he "objected strenuously" to war protestors at home. We didn't believe in amnesty, either. Gary often repeated his feelings about the war in his letters and how he believed American soldiers were fighting for a good cause. His fellow GIs and officers said that Gary did, indeed, die for what he believed in. Gary's direct commanding officer expressed to us that "Gary was what a soldier should be" and told us how helpful he was to the other men in his unit.

As much as Mom, especially, said she didn't like to "brood" about his death, she couldn't be strong all the time. She missed him terribly. She made it known, too, how much she appreciated the kindness of folks here in town when she received the death notice from the Army.

The families of the other boys who died in Vietnam were quick to offer sincere sympathy. But the mothers of these boys became a close, supportive group for each other. At times like these, living in a small town is a blessing. Comfort and understanding are never far away.

~

We were *proud* of Gary. My parents didn't feel bitter or hateful that he chose to defend his country and gave his life in the process. They said Gary wouldn't want them to feel that way. We never really knew Gary's exact location in Vietnam when he died. We all just regretted that the war in Vietnam dragged on as long as it did. So *many* boys were killed. This never should have happened. My parents always told Gary's little girls, Lisa and Kim, to remember their Dad for his bravery and what he did for his country.

My mother especially enjoyed the times Gary wrote her asking my folks to send him canned spaghetti and meatballs. It was one of the things he wanted most. It must have been his "comfort food" in the jungles. We were sure he shared them with the other men. We later found out that they opened the cans with their bayonets.

A Duty to Serve

Dad also had a distinguished military record. From 1940 to 1945 during World War II, he went from a buck private in the air force to a flight engineer on bombers. He probably encouraged Gary to do what he thought was right. Dad did say that he often regretted not making a career of military service. I, too, did a three-year stint in the Army after enlisting. I spent most of my time in Germany.

Gary had always asked us to look after his family if anything ever happened to him. We made that commitment to him. I was the last person to be in touch with Gary's daughters. In 1973 Kim would have been around six-years-old.

"Tell Me About My Father"

Well, Gary and I would go hunting and fishing from time to time. Somehow, I always thought of him as the *quiet* one. (My sisters may have had a different opinion!) We grew up around animals and nature and these were things young boys did. Before and after school, there were always farm chores to do. But, I can't forget the time when we were hunting, and I accidentally shot Gary in the leg with a BB gun. I don't remember who was more surprised! I felt awful.

My sister, Marilee, remembers him as "a real hell raiser". Seeing or chasing a skunk is one thing; *trapping* the animal is quite another. You just know this isn't going to end well, especially if your sister is with you at the time. Both my brother and sister had to take baths in tomato juice to wash off the smell!

On another occasion, Gary and Marilee were walking home from school when Gary decided to use a long branch or some kind of stick to toy with a bee's nest. The bees were not happy, at all. Clouds of bees chased them away as they ran as fast as they could. They were stung so many times we couldn't even count 'em!

Then, there was the time when Gary was in the barn pitching hay. When he finished, he threw the pitchfork down from the second floor of the barn to the ground. Well, it didn't land on hay or dirt, but found Marilee's foot, instead. I don't know if they were accident prone, or if Marilee should have just traveled *alone* more. To this day, she still has the scar. We didn't get a television until she was 10. Maybe if we got one sooner, Marilee would have been watching it instead of spending so much time with Gary, outdoors or in the barn.

My sister, Leslie, thought of Gary as somewhat of a teen rebel. She described him as having piercing eyes and a mischievous smile. She believed that he was searching for who he really was and for his purpose in the world and seemed to find it when he entered the service.

The last picture Leslie had of Gary in Vietnam was one of him eating from a can of spaghetti and meatballs.

"Yes, sometimes we wonder why it had to be Gary. But, so long as he felt as he did, we had made a commitment to back it up."

~ HELEN STYMUS, GARY'S MOTHER

The death of a child—anyone's child—is a life altering experience. Our family knew this. But Mom, our dear Mom, was true to her commitment to Gary and his beliefs. His loss was devastating. Yet, she was proud of the brave son she raised and knew, deep down in her heart, that he didn't die in vain.

CHAPTER FOURTEEN
The Bombing of Cambodia

THE AMERICAN PEOPLE elected Richard M. Nixon President of the United States largely based on his promise to end the nation's involvement in the Viet Nam War. By the time the election came around, the general perception was that there was nothing to be gained by continuing the war, and way too much to lose, particularly in the way of young lives.

At first, Nixon did what he promised, ordering in stages the withdrawal of American soldiers back to the States. However, on April 30, 1970, literally only ten days after appearing on national television to tell the American people that 150,000 soldiers were on their way back home, he again came on TV and reversed course.

Television and technology being what it was in 1970, Mr. Nixon stood behind a dais, written pages neatly in hand, flanked by a flag on each side, and to his back the ruffle of curtains. He started out acknowledging his previous speech, and assuring his audience that those men were indeed coming home. Then reading from those pages Nixon informed the people that the North Vietnamese had established bases within the country of Cambodia from which the Viet Cong and NVA were conducting guerrilla raids on American soldiers and the South. To emphasize his point, he moved away from the dais, and with a pointer in hand, went over to an easel which held a color coded map of Indochina. Indicating a series of red blotches along the Viet Nam/Cambodia border, he showed the nation the audacity of the unscrupulous NVA. As such, he saw no other option than to order an escalation of the conflict and begin the bombing of Cambodia.

The presence of North Vietnamese troops in Cambodia was nothing new. Lyndon B. Johnson and his military advisors were well aware back as far as '65, if not earlier, that the NVA and the VC had been using territory within the borders of the then neutral country for refuge. In response, United States fighter jets had been conducting regular bombing runs as far as 15 miles inside Cambodia.

During this same period, the Khmer Rouge, under the leadership of Pol Pot, was conducting subversive acts against the Cambodian government. Their actions, however, were viewed as little more than a nuisance. The then leader of the country, Prince Sihanouk, counted their number as little more than 5,000. They were poorly armed and lacked the support of the general population.

President Johnson and his advisors, however, viewed the Khmer Rouge as a threat. They were receiving support from the Soviet Union. There was nothing more threatening to Washington at that time than a concern for the spread of Communism. The potential fall of Cambodia was seen as the first domino which would lead to the fall of all of Indochina.

Using the occupation of the North Vietnamese as an excuse, Nixon, under advisement of his military intelligence, made the decision to ignore the policy then in effect, and extended the bombing right up to the outskirts of the capital city of Phnom Penh. In the process, literally hundreds of thousands of square acres of Cambodian land were reduced to craters and burnt waste, and tens of thousands of civilians – perhaps as many as 150,000 – were killed or went missing.

The Khmer Rouge used the bombings to their advantage. Following each attack, they would gather up the local villagers that survived, lead them to the damage, to the dead bodies of their loved ones, and then pointed the finger at the United States. En masse, the surviving villagers became more and more willing to join the Khmer Rouge and take up arms against the US and the Cambodian regime. In no time, the ranks of the Khmer Rouge swelled to more than 200,000. They were then supplied with modern weapons and munitions by both the Chinese and the Soviet Union. The Khmer Rouge overran Phnom Penh in 1973. (1)

Meanwhile, in the States, there was an immediate negative reaction to Nixon's words. Protests erupted throughout the country, but especially on college campuses where students were more aggressive in their opposition. The most prominent of these protests took place at Kent State University in Ohio.

The protests started out no different than any of the others. There were those intently involved, some of whom may not have been students, but outsiders with an agenda, and those who were more or less just spectators. Activity, however, was limited to anti-war speeches and the symbolic burying of an American flag. Later that evening, there were outbursts of violence and vandalism off-campus and in town. In response, the governor of Ohio requested the assistance of the National Guard.

The next day, despite warnings to the contrary, there were further protests on campus. At one point an ROTC building constructed of wood was set afire and burned to the ground. Confrontations escalated between the protestors and the Guard. Tear gas had to be used before the protestors dispersed and some sense of order was restored.

The next day, Sunday, May 3, the protestors again returned. For the most part, rational heads prevailed. However, Governor James Rhodes, who had just flown into the city, inflamed the situation, calling the protestors the worst type of human beings and using language inferring martial law. The informal declaration left the impression that the Guard was now in control of the campus and not university leadership. This impression both emboldened the Guard and enraged the protestors. Tear gas was once again used to disperse the crowds.

On Monday, May 4, student protest leaders called for yet another rally, ignoring the warnings by university leaders that such a rally was prohibited. By noon, more than 3,000 protestors had assembled. Shortly thereafter, a campus policeman, using a bullhorn, attempted to disperse the crowd. He was ignored. He was then put in a National Guard jeep and driven into the mass of people, all the while using the horn ordering the protestors to leave. Instead, he and the Guardsmen accompanying him were met with a hail of stones. They retreated.

At this point, tear gas was again used. The Commander of the Guard, General Canterbury, then ordered his men to lock and load their weapons and move at the back of the crowd to force its retreat.

The protestors were driven up and over Blanket Hill and down into a parking lot on the other side. In the process, the Guard worked itself into the larger part of the crowd and soon found themselves becoming outflanked. Feeling threatened, they reversed direction and started back up to the top of the hill.

Emboldened by the retreat of the Guard, the protestors reversed direction, yelling and throwing rocks. Back at the top of the hill, suddenly and without warning, 28 of the 70 National Guardsmen turned on the crowd and fired. Within a 13 second period, a barrage of over 70 rounds was fired. Four students were killed and nine were wounded. (2)

For many, the Kent State University incident marked the day that the violence of the Viet Nam War had come home.

CHAPTER FIFTEEN

George W. Fischer, Jr.

February 25, 1945 – August 3, 1968

Robert Broekhuizen, Friend

I remember seeing George for the first time on the school bus when we were in grade school. He was never a big kid. And, he couldn't have been more than 13-years-old, when he ducked behind that gas pump, and just disappeared from sight!

Believe me, I wasn't the only one to wonder just how old he was, despite how much he knew about cars. His father owned a 3-bay garage service station in Rochester, so George spent all kinds of hours tinkering and working on cars. He was shorter and maybe not as filled out as the rest of us, but George was way ahead of everyone when it came to cars. The only thing he loved more than regular cars were race stock cars. So did I. And, I think that's why we became such good friends. His dream was to race the stock cars he'd build . . . and he did.

It wasn't unusual for George to come flying out of the garage to pump gas when a customer pulled up. It also gave him an opportunity to talk cars, and fins and tires and bodies and mileage and anything else that rode on four wheels. Like a super revved up engine, George was pumped just being around the sounds and smells of anything automotive.

If you went looking for George after school, on weekends or during any free time he had, you were sure to find him at the family garage, with his head under the hood of a car, or carefully positioned on the *creeper* under it. People said they knew George was at work by the unique, rhythmic sounds he made when he tinkered; the pace of steel-on-steel tools, like the pings and pongs of pinches and chisels and pry bars; and the squeaky turn of a new wrench on a tie rod; or the solid *thwack* that emanated when he capped or uncapped a valve. And, finally, the resounding *zooooom* of a beautiful, supped up engine ignited for her maiden run.

George W. Fischer, Jr. standing next to his father in his three bay service station on Ridge Road in Greece, New York. It was here that George fell in love with cars.

The Ride of Their Lives

When we were juniors at Holley High, George bought his first stock car. He didn't have money for much else. None of us did. But, whatever he had, it went into working on that car. Together, we put hundreds of hours into building the perfect parts for it and soldering like crazy. It was as if we were creating some extra Wonders of the World. Talk about a true labor of love.

George was the leader of it all. We both worked on the cars, but he was the driver when he began racing at Spencer and Lancaster Speedways. And, he won three major races. He took great pride in what he did, and even designed our racing uniforms. They were gold and white. White pants, because the car was white and gold tee shirts, for the gold-painted number 51 on the side of the car. We started off with a '56 Chevy, followed by a '57. The cars were built with a single barrel carburetor and 283-cubic-inch engines. Racing rules said they could be modified up to, but not more than 327 inches.

George, seen standing in front of his first "hot rod", a 1949 Studebaker.

These amazing vehicles needed to be specially maintained. To me, it wasn't the size or power of the engine, but the way the car handled, how it was balanced and its durability. Racing cars were something special. They needed care and attention if we expected them to keep running at peak performance and score well at the end of the year.

~

Everyone knew that Friday nights were Spencer Speedway nights. This speedway held about 300 people. Friday night was a priority. Everything else was second, or third or whatever. The track there was a ½ mile asphalt oval. The typical "heat" race was 13 laps around the track just to warm up. The better a driver did in the heats, the better starting position he earned. This was the moment the excitement really started. I remember feeling like I was actually vibrating from the fearsome growl that 12 to 15 race cars without mufflers made on their first, flat out start. I called it "rolling thunder"! The sound was deafening, but beautiful, like a giant lion roaring to declare his supremacy.

When I close my eyes and let my mind drift back, I remember feeling completely consumed by the frenzy of it all. The towering speedway lights glared down on the track as each car became a blur in those first laps. The anticipation of the race to come was unbearable. The smell of the place was like no other, full of a mixture of gasoline, hot oil, transmission fluid and burning rubber. Every now and then, you'd get a whiff of fresh buttered popcorn or a grilled hot dog smothered in German mustard and kraut, but they couldn't compete with distinctly mechanical aromas of the dizzying race.

On Saturday nights, we upped our game at Lancaster Speedway, which held about 600 people. We raced in the "late model modified" category after paying an entrance fee of $20. Here, the goal was to rack up points during the season and hope to be awarded top prize at the end. Of course, the same "rules" for friends, family and girlfriends applied to Saturdays nights, too. The race came first.

Racing took on a life of its own. We laid down the law to anyone who knew us that racing was *that* important to us. We were a family. It was our own little mini-culture. Racers, pit crews, even girlfriends, all knew and understood that the race was the thing. At the time, I was dating the girl who would become my wife. She knew that every date on a Friday or Saturday night began with her sitting in the grandstand! *After* the race, we'd go out somewhere and have a good time, but the race came first.

If George won—and he did more often than not—we'd be outrageously raucous at the defining moment, then silly and giddy, when the knowledge of a deserved win sank in and our throats were too sore to yell anymore. George, especially, was physically exhausted after a race, but proud to be lauded as a local racing hero. The rest of us were finally able to freely exhale, feel our tight shoulders loosen and our stiff knees unlock . . . and maybe even blink away a tear of joy.

Afterwards, there were lots of hugs and laughter; back slapping and applauding and congratulating from so many people. We knew most of them, but there were always some newcomers who were anxious to introduce themselves and talk to us. Sometimes, kids even asked for our autographs! For a moment in time, we were commanding giants claiming the land as our own. It was a sweet reality.

Most of all, we learned what *growing up* meant for us. Not all life lessons were learned in books or in classrooms. We poured our hearts and minds into this select passion. The sense of accomplishment realized from building something so powerfully durable, with the ability to physically perform seemingly inhuman feats and entertain the viewing public, is barely describable. We built 'em, we drove 'em, we ran 'em to the finish line! The exuberance that comes with this kind of achievement reverberates squarely in your gut. It validates all the work, all the expectation, all the teamwork and it feels better than anything else.

Photo of George waving a checkered flag at his first victory at Spencer Speedway. Note the number 51 on the car.

In just seven days, we'd do it all again.

The Music Men

George and I shared another talent. We both played trumpet in the Holley High School marching band, which gave us more gadgets and instruments to take care of. Believe it or not, the Holley band was named one of the best marching bands in the *country!*

Our music director, Ray Shahin, also played the trumpet in the band and because he was about the same size as George he marched next to him. George kiddingly said that it meant he couldn't goof off! There's a certain precision and coordination required to play in a marching band. Learning to play an instrument was one thing. Walking and playing at the same time, was quite another. Sometimes, just as we were stepping off, George and I would grin to each other. Come to think of it, it was similar, in a way, to building race cars. Maybe it was the way we approached the things we did. We both believed that if you were gonna' do something, you had to do it right. If you believed you could do it, you worked at it and eventually you hoped it would pay off. No one is perfect, but we gave it our best. We really enjoyed showing our stuff in marching band.

Again, we were doing something for the public to see—and hear. We regularly went to state finals and won three times! That's quite a record! The highlight of our time in marching band was being invited to appear and play in the Macy's Thanksgiving Day Parade in New York City. Wow! What an honor that was! I mean, we were *there* in our bright red and black uniforms, looking like *real* toy soldiers! Imagine that. The Holley High School Marching Band heading down Broadway! Tons of people lined the streets, waving and cheering. It was like a dream. And, people watching it on their TVs at home saw us, too. What a feeling. How many people can say they've done something like that? We were lucky kids.

It wasn't just a matter of going to New York City, lining up and marching. It was a major adventure. The parade itself was organized very well. Everyone knew where to be and what to expect. I'll never understand how the organizers of something so huge could pull it off without a hitch. We met so many people from all over and from other schools. There were dancers, and baton twirlers and all the cartoon floats with their huge funny faces suspended from strong cables as they dipped and floated high above the crowd. Television stars and people from Broadway shows rode in beautiful floats.

The neat thing about the parade line-up was that they'd mix it up, so you had a float, then a band, then maybe a cartoon character, then a military band, then a high school band, and so on. Of course, the last float carried Santa Claus, and that really got cheers and applause. I think Macy's actually sponsored that particular float. It figured. People had to do Christmas shopping and Macy's was the perfect place to go! All the store windows along the way were decorated for Christmas. It was really beautiful. I also remember the day being a little chilly, but sunny. It was perfect.

At home, the entire town supported us whenever we competed, but especially leading up to our trip to New York City and after. There were always little expenses you couldn't really predict and our friends and neighbors contributed to that fund. Someone baked oatmeal cookies for us for the bus ride. Another gave us little, handmade Christmas stockings full of candy canes. Little things like that counted. In fact, one year (I don't think it was the Macy's year) the town held a special parade in our honor after we won a state final.

George played the trumpet for Holley's marching band. Here the band is seen marching down 5th avenue in New York City during the 1961 Macy's Thanksgiving Day Parade.

You can't beat the people in your hometown. They see things differently. They just don't stand by and watch; they *do* things. They get involved. They care about each other. Not to say that New York City people weren't nice; there were just so many of them and they always seemed to be busy or in a rush to go someplace else.

It made us proud to be from Holley.

Like a Brother

George practically lived at our house and he was like a son to my mother. His older sister, Pat, always said that George had three Thanksgiving dinners—one with his mother, one with his father (his parents were divorced) and finally, one at my house. It seemed as if he liked that one the best! George could eat and never seem to gain a pound! He always had room for my mother's turkey stuffing. Everything she cooked was good, but I think food tasted better when you shared it with a friend. Simple things like sharing a meal were memorable, happy times.

As our school years went on, we remained solid friends. He even was best man at my wedding. I couldn't imagine anyone else standing up for me. Friendships like ours begin early, when you instinctively lock into the same core beliefs and personal chemistry of a friend you know will be important in your life. Often, close friendships are just enough different and just enough alike to last a lifetime. Many childhood friendships last into young adulthood and ours was like that. It just naturally progressed as we matured. It always felt right. It's comforting to know that even as you grow up and go through life, friendships made early in life still last. When I think back, I can't imagine *not* being friends with George for life. Everybody liked him; and I can say we were *best* friends. If he were here now, I *know* we'd still be best friends, reliving the things we did as kids and going forward with our lives, knowing that the little boys who met on the school bus were still friends, no matter what.

Saluting Number 51

He was only 23-years-old. But, war in some God forsaken place doesn't know that. It only knows that you're the enemy.

You grow up real quick when one of your own dies. George's death hit me really hard. I thought of him as a brother. It was and still is the worst tragedy of my life. It seemed as if he had just left for basic training, and suddenly the army was sending his body home to Holley.

I was numb when I got the news. I couldn't speak. I even thought that I might have misheard the message. The only thing I wondered was what he was doing when it happened. What was his last thought, his last action, his last words to someone who cared? One minute there was life and in a split second it was gone. I hoped it was instantaneous. George would have been alert and kicking; he wouldn't have been inattentive or careless. He'd be the guy we knew and loved until the end.

Your mind gets stuck on the immediacy of the news. You picture him in front of you, and then, you can't and you feel as if you've betrayed him. When you don't expect it, memories surface. And that's the hard part. Something would remind me of George—some word, or movie, or Thanksgiving meal, or how he looked after a race or seeing the present Holly High Marching Band perform—and I'd either smile broadly or fight down tears. Thoughts of George just made me grateful that we shared our lives. I'd think of how he laughed; how he talked; how his interests were contagious; how loyal and caring he was and how I couldn't picture a better friend. How lucky I was to know him. I was sure that wherever he was in the great beyond, he was loved.

Part of Me

Shortly afterwards, I moved to Michigan and have lived there most of my life since college. My wife and I still have family in Holley and we make it a point to visit home every year around the Christmas holidays. Some people plan a vacation to destinations like Hawaii or Mexico, the Bahamas, or even Europe. We are perfectly content going back to Holley. In a way, we *need* to. Our lives there are forever part of us in a unique way that defines small town living.

Holley relaxes and comforts us; it is familiar, and at the same time, different than the early years we knew growing up there. The last time I was there, I noticed that the fountain in the town square was now working. The town council had voted to spend the money to get the fountain back in working order. That's a good thing! It showed that the town I knew and still love, cares.

It's where we were born, raised, schooled and learned what every kid learns: core values and beliefs, commitment to helping and valuing others, supporting the endeavors of our neighbors and buoying each other up in both triumphant and heartbreaking circumstances.

Most important, it is *still* George's home, even as he rests in Sandy Creek Cemetery. He is an important, unforgettable part of my life.

~

Patricia (Fischer) Nelson, Sister

Our family was thoroughly devastated. Sadly, our story would be relived countless times over across the country and especially in Holley. Townspeople were so generous and supportive. They sent cards, offered masses, sent food. Mostly, they sent a collective kind of love and buffering against the reality that no one, *no one*, was exempt from this kind of hell. If this could happen here, it could happen anywhere.

After our bunch of friends had arrived and expressed condolences to our family, most of us sat in silence at the Merrill-Grinnell Funeral Home; some of us were too shocked to pray or do whatever one was supposed to do at the funeral of your brother. Our parents and relatives came. It felt like the entire town of Holley turned out to offer kindness and understanding—anything to soften the blow of senseless loss. That's what we do.

I was angry and unbelieving. My brother George died for our country, and I felt completely useless. Why was I even there? I looked at my friends—*our* friends—and nobody seemed to know what to do or what to feel. It brought the war to our door. We simply hadn't lived long enough to know what to do at the funeral of someone so vital to our lives. George knew what to do half a world away, and he died trying to accomplish whatever his job was. I doubt that he believed we should have even been there, but he'd do his job. He didn't have a choice. Nothing in our lives could compare to that.

Good Vibrations

Mom looked up momentarily. I saw her take a deep breath and exhale slowly. She was weary. The tissue she held in her hand was reduced to a small, soggy white ball.

We talked of the countless stray dogs George had smuggled into our back yard. George beamed each time he brought one home and our family just melted—mostly because George was so committed to taking care of little, helpless lives. We came to believe that they actually knew they were in the good hands of this kind, sweet-natured rescuer. His smile and the accomplished look on his face said, "I've saved another one!"

Then, there was that pathetic one-legged chicken he found. No one knew where or how George came upon it, but it, too, found a home at George's impromptu animal hospital in our back yard. We never knew if the chicken's actual medical condition was, in fact, being without a leg or something else. It didn't matter to George. He was on a mission to nurse it back to health. He was just that sort of individual—a caring steward of living things, even at an early age. Everyone thought he'd surely become a veterinarian one day.

~

We were all hugging someone, even Mom and Dad after being divorced for several years had to hold on to each other, when suddenly a slight tremor reverberated through the floor. Outside, the sky was a bright blue. There wasn't a lazy cloud to be seen anywhere. It couldn't be the beginning of a storm?

People began to rise uneasily from their chairs, take a few steps, and then cock their heads to listen for another rumble. Yes. *Oh, yes.* Whatever was happening seemed to cut a path right down Geddes Street and idle in front of the funeral home. Holley had never had an earthquake! This sounded like something out of a sci-fi movie. . . or maybe we were under attack!

Boxes of tissue strategically placed in the room staggered toward the edges of small, tasteful tables and silently began dropping to the floor. The petals of the fresh, sweet smelling flowers in the funeral arrangements also began to quiver rhythmically. I thought that if anything terrible was about to happen, it would have already descended upon this room. I was the first to dart for the door. I was going to fight off whatever intended to spoil this gathering. I flung my shoulder against the long, metal bar on the door, and as it cracked open, a big number 51 came into view. It seemed to be suspended at least 15-feet up in the air.

A small, curious, and somewhat worried group had gathered behind me. I turned quickly and caught the expressions on the faces of a few of the guys we grew up with. They didn't look worried at all. In fact, their eyes were bright and they were grinning from ear-to-ear. They *got* it! I threw the door open full force and couldn't believe what I saw.

There, in a deafening, growling, honorable procession down Geddes Street, were at least six old farm trucks driven by racing friends. In the back of each monster truck was a carefully and proudly mounted stock car. Emblazoned on the side of each car was a gold-colored number *51*, George's old racing number. Incredibly, each of George's old racing buddies had painted the number on the sides of their racing cars to honor George at his funeral. It's a sight I will never forget.

Members of the Holley police, also in attendance, followed the drivers and escorted them to the official funeral home parking lot, which was barely able to accommodate the humongous vehicles.

Nothing was too great for George.

CHAPTER SIXTEEN

The End Game

WHILE THE END OF THE VIETNAM WAR is generally associated with the fall of Saigon in April of 1975, negotiations for a settlement had actually begun much earlier. By 1965, as many as five different countries had taken initiative to bring an end to the US bombing of North Vietnam. Those countries were Rumania, Sweden, Norway, France, and Italy. The US even had names for each of these efforts: Packers for the Rumanian efforts, Aspen for Sweden, Ohio for Norway, Pennsylvania for France, and Killy for Italy.

The Rumanians had only one objective: Cease the bombing in North Vietnam. At one point, they even went so far as to say—inaccurately—that they had received direct word from the North Vietnamese Government that it was ready to negotiate. However, as the bombing was still going on, and the US was well aware that cessation of the bombing was not only a priority for the North, but an absolute, neither side placed much stock in the Packers negotiations.

The Swedes were perceived more for wanting to take credit for bringing an end to the war than actually doing anything to bring about that end. Regardless, by the end of 1967, the Government of Sweden was perceived by South Vietnam as cozying up to the North, thereby alienating themselves from one of the key participants in the process. The Swedish effort fell apart shortly thereafter.

Norway's role in the peace process never gained much traction. Although, like Sweden, its general population was anti-American as far as the war went, and the country generally remained neutral with regard to Hanoi. The Government of North Vietnam saw this neutrality as siding with the South, and therefore showed no interest in Norway's efforts.

The French effort remained consistent and strong throughout the early attempts at a settlement. Hanoi was satisfied with what was referred to as the 'no advantage' position proposed by the French, meaning that the US would not be afforded any degree of leverage during the process not afforded to the North Vietnamese. Regardless, talks were slow to materialize.

The Italians were less concerned with the actual negotiations than with an actual settlement, insisting on terms which guaranteed a self-sufficient and strong Government of South Vietnam. It was only when there was a clear picture of what this meant did the Italians believe any agreement between the US and the Hanoi could be hammered out. Killy fell apart following the end of the Tet Offensive when the Italians warned Hanoi that any further actions on their part would kill the deal. In response, Ambassador Su of North Vietnam said, "From the moment the two sides met, it was obvious no such thing could happen."

Despite these efforts by the world community to bring about peace, Hanoi was telling its population that there could be only one acceptable outcome: A decisive and final victory in which all of Vietnam was under the control of Hanoi. Fighting would go on throughout the negotiation process. The following communication sent from the DRV (Democratic Republic of Vietnam) to the US in 1967 provides insight into its position:

The position of the Government of the Democratic Republic of Viet-Nam is that the United States should cease indefinitely and without conditions the bombing and all other acts of war against the Democratic Republic of Viet-Nam. It should withdraw

American troops and satellites from South Viet-Nam, recognize the National Liberation Front of South Viet-Nam and let the Vietnamese people themselves regulate their internal affairs. It is only after the unconditional stopping of bombing and all other acts of war against the Democratic Republic of Viet-Nam, that it would be possible to engage in conversations. (Pentagon Papers, Part VI. C. 4.)

Lyndon B. Johnson, then the President of the US, responded before the National Legislative Conference in a way which illustrated the distrust between the two nations:

As we have told Hanoi time and time again, the heart of the matter is this: The United States is willing to stop all aerial and naval bombardment of North Vietnam when this will lead promptly to productive discussions. We, of course, assume that while discussions proceed, North Vietnam would not take advantage of the bombing cessation or limitation. (Pentagon Papers, Part VI. C. 4.)

The result was eight years of stalemate filled with on-going military actions on both sides. (1)

In August of '67, the US temporarily ceased bombardment of Hanoi. Despite the ceasefire, the North Vietnamese forces continued to push into South Vietnam.

On September 25, a communiqué was sent by Henry Kissinger, via proxy, to Mai Van Bo, the North Vietnamese chief negotiator in France. In it he expressed five specific concerns, one of which was that Washington and Hanoi were having "great difficulty understanding each other's thought processes." Washington was under the impression that a cessation to the bombing would result simultaneously in a sit-down with Hanoi. That didn't take place.

Secret Peace Talks Begin

From August '69 through August '71, Kissinger engaged in 'secret negotiations' with Le Duc Tho, an influential official with the Government of the Democratic Republic of Viet-Nam. What made the negotiations 'secret' was that South Viet-Nam was not included.

Kissinger and Tho met twelve times in Paris. Throughout these meetings, Hanoi insisted on a complete cessation of all military action on the part of the US and a complete withdrawal of all US and South Vietnamese forces from North Viet-Nam, Cambodia, and Laos. There would be no further negotiations until this condition was met.

For its part, the US insisted on a stop to the infiltration of the South by the North.

Both sides agreed to a simultaneous release of all prisoners of war. Hanoi further insisted on the ousting of the then President of South Viet-Nam, Nguyen Van Thieu, for someone more sympathetic with the NLF.

Ultimately, the proposal hit an impasse. The US refused to remove by process a leader the DRV failed to remove by force, and the DRV refused to cease the infiltration of the South, holding the position that the NLF was the legitimate and favored voice of the people.

On March 30, 1972, Hanoi responded by launching the Eastertide Offensive, an all-out invasion of the South with a force of more than 200,000 soldiers. Hanoi's objective was not only to split South Viet-Nam, but in the process embarrass the US forces, and in doing so thwart Nixon's re-election. Nixon was seen as an obstacle to an end to the fighting.

President Nixon responded by ordering a renewed and intensified bombing of North Vietnam, saying privately, "The bastards have never been bombed like they're going to be bombed this time." For the next two weeks, B-52 bombers penetrated as far as 145 miles into North Viet-Nam. Both Hanoi and the harbor at Haiphong were hit.

On April 27, the peace talks resumed. Nevertheless, heavy fighting continued in both the South and the North, with the North taking one key city after another. At this point both the US and South Viet-Nam pulled out of the peace talks.

The second week of May, despite world condemnation, Nixon ordered 125 additional warplanes to Viet-Nam. Immediately upon arrival, intense bombing was directed at all key roads, bridges, and facilities in and around North Vietnam. The harbor was mined. These actions signaled the start of Operation Linebacker.

Due to Operation Linebacker, which cut off supplies coming in from the north, the ARVN managed to regain some momentum. An attack on An Loc was beaten back by the South with help from US B-52s. Two other counter-offensives drove the North from two key provinces.

Acknowledging the effectiveness of Operation Linebacker, in which over 125,000 tons of bombs were dropped and more than 100,000 North Vietnamese soldiers killed, peace talks in Paris resumed. At the same time, General Giap was quietly removed as commander of all DRV forces.

Concessions

On October 8, 1972, before the Presidential election, Henry Kissinger and Le Duc Tho met again in Paris with each making concessions. The US agreed to allow North Vietnamese troops to remain in South Viet-Nam, and Hanoi to allow Thieu to remain in power. Thieu condemned the agreement saying, at least for the South, it amounted to surrender. Following the election, Nixon, in a letter to Thieu, assured the president that if the North in any way failed to abide by the conditions of the cease fire, the US would take immediate military action.

On October 26, Kissinger went on national television and in a speech of few words told the nation, contrary to the expectations of Nixon, "We believe peace is at hand." It wasn't.

By late November, all US troops have been removed from Viet-Nam. Only 16,000 MACV members remained to act as military advisors to the ARVN.

Unfortunately, two weeks later, Kissinger was obligated to

present to Le Duc Tho a list of 69 additional conditions demanded by President Thieu. Tho, on behalf of Hanoi, rejected those conditions, and the peace talks again collapsed.

Nixon, as he had promised, gave Hanoi only 72 hours to return to the table. Hanoi chose not to respond. Nixon ordered the commencement of Operation Linebacker II. Over the next eleven days, an additional 100,000 bombs were dropped on Hanoi.

The second week of January '73, Hanoi relented, and Le Duc Tho returned to the Paris peace talks with Kissinger. Under the terms, the US agreed to halt all military actions in the country, 150,000 North Vietnamese soldiers were permitted to remain in the South, and Thieu continued as the president. However, the country remained split, and South Viet-Nam essentially had two separate governments: one run by Thieu and the other by the NLF.

Gerald Ford was sworn in as U.S. president on 9 August 1974 after President Nixon resigned due to the Watergate scandal. Ford told the American people, "Our long national nightmare is over."

At the start of 1975, the South Vietnamese had three times the artillery and twice the number of tanks and armored cars as the North. They also had 1,400 aircraft and a two-to-one numerical superiority in combat troops over them. However, they faced a well-organized, highly determined and well-funded North Vietnam. Much of the North's material and financial support came from the communist bloc. Within South Vietnam, there was increasing chaos. The departure of the American military had compromised an economy heavily dependent on U.S. financial support and the presence of a large number of U.S. troops.

The End Game

On 10 March 1975, General Dung launched Campaign 275, a limited offensive into the Central Highlands, supported by tanks and heavy artillery. The South Vietnamese Army proved incapable of resisting the onslaught, and its forces collapsed on 11 March. Hanoi was surprised by the speed of their success.

President Thiêu, fearful that his forces would be cut off in the north by the Communists ordered a retreat. The president declared this to be a "lighten the top and keep the bottom" strategy. But the withdrawal soon turned into a bloody rout.

In the United States, the war was perceived as doomed. President Ford gave a televised speech on 23 April, declaring an end to U.S. aid in Vietnam. North Vietnamese tanks breached defenses on the outskirts of Saigon. In the early morning hours of 30 April, the last U.S. Marines evacuated the embassy by helicopter, as civilians swamped the perimeter and poured onto the grounds. Many of them had been employed by the Americans and were left to their fate.

On 30 April 1975, NVA troops entered the city of Saigon and quickly overcame all resistance, capturing key buildings and installations. A tank from the 324th Division crashed through the gates of the Independence Palace at 11:30 a.m. local time and the Viet Cong flag was raised. (2)

The Vietnam War was over.

CHAPTER SEVENTEEN

Paul S. Mandracchia

November 3, 1951-April 14, 1970

TODD DEFRANK, FRIEND

PAUL LOOKED KIND OF HYPNOTIZED for a minute.

"Hey. *Paul.* What are you looking at?" I asked.

"Huh?"

I gave him a jab in the ribs with my elbow.

"Earth to Paul. Do you *know* her?"

"I'm not sure."

"Hey, Romeo, either you do or you don't!"

Paul turned to me for the first time since he laid eyes on Michelle and said, "Well, I'm *going* to!"

Great, I thought to myself. He's in love. Now, what am I supposed to do?

He looked as if someone had cast a spell over him. I guess when it feels natural, it just happens. Paul walked right up to Michelle and began talking. It didn't look like she was there with anyone, except a couple of girlfriends. (Maybe I could dance with one of *them*.)

"Hi. I'm Paul," he said, without a hint of shyness.

"What's your .... '

"I'm Michelle," she said, overlapping his question.

"You look nice," he said.

"Thanks. You look nice, too," she said blushing a little.

"Do you go to Holley?"

"No, Kendall," said Michelle.

"Yeah, I have friends who go there," Paul said.

They laughed awkwardly. Michelle's girlfriends fluttered around them, probably thinking they were inconspicuous. They weren't.

Finally! The music started!

The opening notes of the Doors' "Light My Fire" started up. Kids paired off, and started to dance. Paul smiled at Michelle and took her hand. I think his fire had just started! Paul looked so darn happy. "A Whiter Shade of Pale" by Procol Harum followed. Wow! A *slow* dance! How lucky could a guy get?

I asked a couple of the girls I knew from school to dance, but mostly hung out a lot on the sides with my guy friends slurping down pop pretending it was beer.

Well, it wasn't Jim Morrison who won Michelle's heart that night; it was my buddy Paul. As the lights blinked a few times signaling the end of the dance, Michelle was writing something on a very small piece of paper, which she eagerly handed to Paul.

It was her phone number.

Michelle and Paul started seeing each from that night, on.

Paul and I grew up in Holley. There are a lot of woods, orchards and farmland in the area. He was a year older than I, and was one of my best friends. We did everything together and hung out a lot. Sometimes we would go hunting, fishing and swimming. I remember eating dinner at his parents' house. There was always lots of good food there. The thing I remember the most though were the dances in Albion at the Oak Orchard Bowling Alley. That was when Paul met a girl by the name of Michelle. He started going out with her and we sort of lost touch.

I was a junior in high school then. I was hanging out with another group of friends and was into sports a lot that year. I heard Paul joined the Marine Corps and had gone to Vietnam…

"L'America!"

Rosa Aliberti, Paul's Great Aunt

You had to want it bad. The trip to America, that is.

Even today, the trip by boat from Sciacca, Italy, on Palermo's seacoast, to the port of Naples, is an overnight journey, lasting anywhere from 8 to 10 and a half hours, depending on the ferry company you choose. Imagine what this undertaking was like for Sicilians leaving their mother country for a better life in America in the early 1900s! They were really brave. Once the decision was made, there was no turning back.

~

My aunt and uncle, Louie and Rosalie Mandracchia, knew exactly how it felt as they sailed out of Naples on the *Principe de Piemonte,* bound for New York in 1910. Maybe the people they met on the boat to Naples also boarded the ship to New York, or maybe not, because these ships stopped at other European cities, too, to discharge or take on more passengers.

But surely, this vessel that would cross the Atlantic was packed with Italians looking for the same things—a stable government, jobs, a physically healthy environment, a safe place to raise a family and more. Isn't that what everyone wants?

By the late 19th century, the Italian peninsula and the rest of the country were united under one flag, but it wasn't *unified,* if that makes sense. After years of political splintering and uprisings, the social climate in Sicily had been degraded through crime, violence, and widespread poverty. Natural disasters, like an erupting volcano—Mount Etna—and diseases like malaria and tuberculosis made people want to escape. People in the southern part of Italy, Sicilians, were basically poor peasants who worked the land, without means or access to ways of improving their lives. That's where our family is from. For so many, the dream of reaching "L'America" became a job in itself and families began to set aside whatever money they had to make their move. (1)

The Crossing

So, they sailed, along with my cousins and great aunt to America on the ocean liner, *Principe di Piemonte*. The ship was actually built in 1907 by a Scottish company, Sir J. Laing & Sons, Ltd, for the Italian line, Lloyd Sabaudo. For its time, this ship was well-equipped with four masts and two funnels, the ship's smokestacks. Two other liners—the Re d'Italia and the Regina d'Italia—were built by the same company for the Italian line. They were known as the three sister ships, identical in every way. But, the Principe could carry more.

Her history is interesting. She was sold three times. In 1913, she was renamed the Principello, with service between Rotterdam and New York; in 1914 she was sold to the Canadian Northern's Royal Line, which sailed from Canada to Bristol, England, and in 1916, she was bought by the Cunard Company and renamed the *Folia*, which shipped goods between Liverpool and New York, only. (2)

It couldn't have been an easy trip. It took about three weeks to cross the Atlantic, give or take time depending on weather and sea conditions. I wonder if they made friends quickly. I wonder if they got sick or seasick. Were they too anxious to eat or sleep? From what I know of them, I'm sure they were social—but a little cautious. And, I bet a lot of conversation went on about why they left, how they made a living and where they lived before. Immediate family made these trips, often leaving other relatives behind. When people got settled, they'd send money back to Italy and plan to bring other family over, too. That's the thing about Italians. It's all about *la famiglia!*

The only thing Uncle Louie and Aunt Rosalie knew at the time was that this ship was going to bring them and all their meager worldly belongings to a new world and a new life.

"Now, We're In America!"

The first thing you see as you come into the harbor is a single beacon of light, held high in the air. As a New Yorker *and* as an Italian American, to this day, nothing is more powerful than seeing the Statue of Liberty slowly materialize as your boat makes a crescent curve into more shallow waters and she looms large and strong before your eyes.

Although she represents American freedom, many people don't know the details of the statue. She represents Libertas, a Roman goddess. She holds a tablet containing the date of the American Declaration of Independence (July 4, 1776) and a broken chain lies at her feet. Very symbolic.

After sailing across the Atlantic Ocean for almost a month, with plenty of time to think, re-think, maybe doubt, and hope a whole lot, the sight of Miss Liberty guiding the paths of European immigrants into New York harbor has got to be an unforgettable, once in a lifetime experience. I can picture my Uncle Louie, saying something like, "*Now,* we're in L'America!" It made it official.

I've spoken to people who just come to visit New York, and they say that the moment the Statue of Liberty comes into view, everyone stops talking in a kind of silent respect and awe. Many whip out their cameras. Many cry. Many thank God they are free. (3)

L'Isola dell Lagrime: Ellis Island

Ellis Island was intended to be a good thing. Although, when it first opened in 1892, new immigrants were terribly confused and frightened by the strict procedures and paperwork routines necessary before they were cleared to go on to their American destinations. In its early days, Ellis Island was overrun with pickpockets, thieves, and con men. It must have felt like a mini-prison. What an eye opener! Eventually, the federal government restructured the immigrant process and built temporary living space for detained immigrants.

The Mandracchias arrived at Ellis Island in 1910. Now they were Americans!

Everyone heard about the stringent medical exams immigrants received. Overall, it seemed as if some inspectors were a little too ready to reject people, for minor medical reasons, such as failing an eye exam, or having a cough, or seeming too frail to work. I understand that less than two percent of Italians were actually turned away, while others feared being separated from their families for any reason. Because of this possibility, some called Ellis Island "l'isola dell lagrime", the Island of Tears.

It closed in 1932. (4)

Just Like Home, But Better

"Around the corner came a band of musicians with green cock-feathers in hats set rakishly over fierce, sunburnt faces. A raft of boys walked in front, abreast of two bored policemen, stepping in time to the music. Four men carried a silk-fringed banner with evident pride. Behind them a strange procession toiled along: women with babies at the breast and dragging little children; fat and prosperous padrones carrying their canes like staves of office and authority; young men out for a holiday; old men with lives of hardship and toil written in their halting gait and worn and crooked frames…"

Description of an Italian "festa" by New York Police Commissioner Theodore Roosevelt in Century Magazine, 1899

It was the norm for Italian immigrants to form the same kinds of small, distinct cultural communities in America as they had in Italy. You had sections of "Calabrese", "Siciliana", "Napolitano" and so forth living in parts of New York; in the Bronx, Brooklyn, and New Jersey towns close to Lower Manhattan. The greatest numbers of immigrants settled in Manhattan, specifically on and around the famous Mulberry Street. This is the section of New York named Little Italy.

Immigrants quickly settled there, as they became part of the working population. They were street vendors, store and business owners and residents, who all spoke Italian with their own dialects and tended to cluster in separate neighborhoods. The population of a village in Italy could have ended up living on the same block in New York, in the same tenement buildings, where they kept the dynamics of their lives in "the old country" still going on in New York. This included their religion, socializing, maintaining grudges (unfortunately) and social standing. This clannish behavior was called "campanilismo", which, in Italy, referred to showing loyalty to people living within the sound of village (or city) church bells. (5)

~

Uncle Louie and Aunt Rosalie Mandracchia settled in Brooklyn. There they owned and operated *Pop Louie's Fish Market* for many, many years. I wonder if they ever did business in the legendary Fulton Fish Market section of Brooklyn. Many Italians worked there, too.

For Uncle Louie, he still lived near water as he had in Italy; he still spoke his native language; he still lived with Italian customs; *but* the big difference was that he was making real money! It was just like home, only better!

By the 1920s and 30s, Italian immigrants had, for the most part, adjusted to life in America and so did their children. Some still wanted to hold on to the old ways. Their kids went to public schools, learned English, learned to identify with a new flag, associated with other kids in schoolyards and sometimes even ended up with a new American sounding name. These kids were second generation Italian Americans and often disagreed with the way their parents still wanted to hold on to the old ways.

I'm 84 now. I still think of those 'old' days.

"Bob"

Leslie Mandracchia, Paul's Brother

My father, Onofrio Roberto Mandracchia, was a character with a colorful life. Let's just say he wasn't your typical second generation kid. One of the first things he did was "Americanize" himself real quick. In an instant, he became *"Bob"*! He stuck with it and everyone knew him that way. I never knew what happened between him and his parents, but according to my Aunt Rose, my father upped and left home at 15 to join a carnival. Can you imagine that? It sounds like a fiction story, but it's all true!

He did have a good skill and that was cooking. It really set him apart from other guys. After he took off with the carnival, he eventually ended up in Idaho of all places, and worked as a cook for a mining camp. In 1935 the Social Security Act was passed. My father applied for a Social Security card and became an official, card carrying American.

In World War II he joined the army and was sent to England. Again, he spent the entire war in England cooking! His commanding general liked his cooking so much that he never sent him to Europe to fight in the war. It was in England where he met my mother Norah.

Where Is Your Gas Mask? WWII in England

According to my mother, when World War II broke out in England, the English people proved they were strong, determined and, for the most part, unified against Adolph Hitler and his German forces.

Every aspect of British life was "mobilized", sustaining a strong wartime spirit that spread to and included all class barriers. For civilians like my mother and her family, bombings by air of towns and cities during the Blitz were expected and feared. Life revolved around these dangerous attacks. In the ensuing five years, statistics of the casualties were staggering. In all, over 60 thousand British civilians were killed and over 86 thousand were seriously injured. One of my mother's cousins was killed during one of these attacks.

Air raid drills were commonly held to prepare civilians as to what they had to do when bombings actually took place. Sirens would wail as the lights of bomber planes flickered in the skies of English cities and the countryside. No matter what you were doing or where you were, you needed to find shelter for safety. Above all, at all times you needed to carry and use your gas mask if/when necessary.

In 1940, food rationing began—particularly of meats, sugar,

tea and coffee—dividing amounts equally for use by adults and children. Imported, non-food items like textiles, soap and fuel, as in English "petrol", were also rationed. The rationing of clothing followed in 1941. My mother said these were tough times but everyone held together. She said it was funny, it actually made people stronger.

Half a million women joined the English military and/or worked in factories. My mother worked at a button factory. One out of 10 men enlisted. Others—both men and women—were outwardly recruited for factory jobs that supported the war effort and men were recruited to work in the coal mines.

English life in wartime held very few, if any, luxuries or common social pleasures. Your time, whereabouts and activities were gauged in this national mobilization effort to keep people as safe as possible.

The evacuation of approximately three million people was achieved throughout the war, moving people beyond the reach of German bombings. At the outbreak of war, German and Austrian "aliens" were considered high risk and were held in political custody immediately and indefinitely. Italy joined the war in 1940 in support of the Germans.

The Evacuation of Dunkirk

In May of 1940, Germany invaded France and Belgium and pushed the British Expeditionary Force back to the French port of Dunkirk. The British Royal Navy launched Operation "Dynamo", named for the massive electric generator sitting in the English war room which was situated inside the cliffs of Dover. There, under the direction of Admiral Bertram Ramsey, the evacuation of all troops from the beaches of Dunkirk, was planned and accomplished, bringing those forces safely back to Britain.

The last British troops were evacuated in June, crossing the English Channel as French forces covered their transport. Prime Minister Winston Churchill expected that it would be possible to rescue only 20,000 to 30,000 men. A total of approximately 338,000 were rescued.

Germany Surrenders

Adolph Hitler committed suicide on April 30, 1945. His successor, Grand Admiral Karl Donitz, negotiated an end to the war with Britain and its Allies. On May 4, 1945, British Field Marshal Bernard Montgomery accepted the unconditional surrender of German forces in the Netherlands, northwest Germany and Denmark. On May 7, 1945, Supreme Allied Commander General Dwight D. Eisenhower accepted the unconditional surrender of all German forces at his headquarters in Reims, France. German General Alfred Jodl signed the document on behalf of Germany. Josef Stalin, leader of Soviet allied troops, requested his own official ceremony. This took place in Berlin on May 8, 1945. Yet another unconditional surrender was signed by German Field Marshal William Keitel. This phase of the war in Europe had ended. Yet, the war with Japan did not end until August of 1945. My parents were married one month later. (6)

September 5, 1939 – Getty Images

On the Holley Home Front

The very same talent that kept my father out of the war continued at home in Holley, where we guessed that it was his outstanding peanut brittle recipe that kept him safe and alive in England!

For Italians, food and *famiglia* always go together. To this day, I remember his most popular dishes were Spanish rice, his sauce and meatballs (of course!), a variety of cakes and homemade cornbread. He just had a way of cooking practically anything that wasn't nailed down.

Speaking of "nailed down", when he took Paul and me fishing, he'd cook whatever we caught; usually bull heads and smelts. This was really cheap fishing and cheap eating. But, Dad could make a feast very economically. He got ample use out of a special "tenderizer" which he used on the bull heads. For those who don't know this fish, it's basically a variety of catfish. Anyway, his tenderizer was a hefty piece of wood with a big *nail* attached to it. He'd pound those bullheads until they were tender and ready to cook. After he got through with them, they were delicious! He also prepared and cooked the deer we shot, and made tasty collard greens for "the blacks". My mother made more "civilized" meals of steaks, kidney pies, roast beef and lamb.

Sicily II

We always laughed about how the Mandracchia family created Sicilys wherever they went. Grandpa Louie began our family history in Brooklyn, so we called Canarsie Sicily I. When my father finally ended up in Holley, we called it Sicily II.

By the late 19th, early 20th century, Rochester, New York was considered to be one of the fastest growing cities in the United States. My aunt had already settled in Holley and urged her brother (Bob) to move there. Once more, the Italian population in Holley stuck together. Many of the men were skilled laborers; in this case as masons, and we have them to thank for the durable buildings downtown, many of which still stand.

~

To say that my father was a bit of a wheeler-dealer, is an understatement. Yes, he was always a hard worker, but could never pass up a chance to place a bet somewhere.

We never asked how he got it, but he'd show up trading two cases of Duffey-Mott grape juice for tickets to get us into the horse track in Batavia. He loved this! He'd bet on all the races. Everyone played the numbers in those days and everyone knew how to contact Holley's four or five busy bookies. I mean, by betting just $2, you stood a chance of winning $250!

My father was a hands-on guy and *always* worked. He couldn't sit still. He smoked two to three packs of cigarettes a day and probably drank 20 cups of coffee a day. I don't remember him drinking much alcohol; maybe he'd have a few beers now and then. But, even when he was at Duffey-Mott doing his job, if the roof leaked, they'd hire him to fix it. If someone's barn door flapped open and wouldn't stay closed, he'd fix it. If someone wanted their house painted, he'd paint it.

Aunt Rosa always reminded us that he weighed only 125 pounds when he got married. Forty years later when he retired, he still weighed 125 pounds. Despite the fact that my father was always on the go, I'd describe him as calm and peaceful—even for a Sicilian! But, when he did get angry, like Mt. Etna ... look out!

I think Paul probably inherited the calm and peaceful side of my father, especially when he played his guitar.

~

April 2, 1970

Dear Mom,

Just to let you know I'm alright. I got your package. Just pick from the list I mentioned in my last letter then you'll know what to send me in the future ok? Anyway it looks like we're staying out in the bush for awhile and I don't know when I'll be able to write again.

I am thinking what did you tell Michelle? She wrote something about it in her last letter to me but she wouldn't tell me. Maybe you will.

I like her very much mom. I've never missed anyone as much as her, and you and dad, and home.

Love, Paul

Paul pictured with his parents after graduating from Marine boot camp. His parents met in England where his dad was stationed leading up to the invasion of Normandy during World War II.

"Dear Mr. & Mrs. Mandracchia . . ."

"It is with profound regret that I write to you concerning the recent death of your son, Lance Corporal Paul S. Mandracchia, U.S. Marine Corps on April 6, 1970. His death is a source of sorrow to me and his many friends in the company.

On April 5 while in their night Platoon Patrol Base the enemy silently crept up to Paul's Position and a number of grenades were thrown towards his fighting hole. Six Marines were wounded and evacuated. Paul died at the Station Hospital as a result of his wounds.

Paul was awarded posthumously the Gallantry Cross with Palm by the South Vietnamese Government for "Accomplishing deeds of valor and displaying heroic conduct while fighting the enemy".

Paul was posthumously awarded the Vietnamese Cross for Gallantry for "accomplishing deeds of valor and displaying heroic conduct while fighting the enemy". Paul was the last boy from Holley to die in Vietnam.

Paul won the respect of all who knew him by his eagerness to help and his devotion to duty. He was a fine young man and an outstanding Marine. We hope the knowledge that your son is missed and displayed tremendous bravery will in some measure; lessen the suffering caused by your great loss.

Sincerely,

David R. Johnson, Capt.

For Holley, the war in Vietnam was finally over.

CONCLUSION

On April 30, 2015, the Vietnamese people celebrated the 40th anniversary of the fall of Saigon to North Vietnam. Marking the historic event as a "celebration" for the now-unified country, encompassed a dual message: North Vietnam was victorious over American forces and, in the process, also quelled its own civil strife.

Vietnam 40 Years later

Three-million Vietnamese and over 58,000 Americans died in this war; yet, many people in Vietnam, united under Communist rule, still remain unsettled and confused over the civil and social outcomes of the conflict.

The most dramatic outcome focused on the country's growing economy, as capitalists and burgeoning entrepreneurs jumped on opportunities to bring cosmopolitan wealth and trendy Western culture to Saigon. Chanel and Cartier boutiques, to name a few, quickly lined the streets, along with specialized coffee cafes and upscale tattoo parlors.

Business owners—many of them in their mid-20s and early 30s—have preferred locating in Saigon instead of Hanoi in the north, where businesses are approved or given the go-ahead based on personal and/or political leanings.

To these people, looking ahead, rather than at Vietnam's stormy political past, is the better choice. For them, this anniversary was meaningless. They are more intent on participating in Vietnam's economic success now and in the future.

However, according to Huy Duc, Vietnamese author of *The Winning Side*, the only way for Vietnam to move forward economically and politically at the end of the war, was to explore and understand varying perspectives as to why there was a war in the first place. In his view, the great majority of Vietnamese people were never clear on exactly why the war was fought.

Duc concluded, "Both sides have to agree on what happened... People who were sent from the North believed that they fought against the invading Americans and were liberating the South. And many people from the South ... believed it was a civil war, that the South was invaded by the North."

The most noticeable change after the Communists settled into power was not noticeable at all. In fact, it seemed like business as usual—the business-like details of war still prevailed. Many South Vietnamese officers, for example, were sent to "re-education camps" for more than a decade, doing hard labor, while they were separated from their wives and families.

How did this unite the traditionally troubled division of North and South Vietnam?

"After the war, the winning side did nothing to reconcile the people," said Duc. "They dug the divisions deeper and deeper. So reconciliation has now become more difficult than on the day of April 30, (1975). So the thing we have to do is not only unify the different parts of the country but also unify people's hearts."

Holley 40 Years Later

"We are today remembering those soldiers, past and present, who gave their lives so that we, their families, friends and neighbors, may continue to enjoy

our precious freedom. May we continue to remember, year after year, that freedom is not free. And may we long continue to thank and honor our United States soldiers."

~ *John Kenney, Mayor of Holley, May 26, 2014*

As the town of Holley observed Memorial Day in 2014, the sentiments of its military community and residents remained steady and unchanged. In addition to speeches, the placing of memorial wreaths, a parade and cemetery services honoring all veterans from Holley who gave their lives in service to our country, military officials reiterated the driving, unchanging element behind this kind of patriotism: the concept of freedom.

Referring to the oath taken by ROTC students at the Rochester Institute of Technology, Major Ryan D'Andrea emphasized the following:

"The oath is to the Constitution, the ideals on which this nation was founded, not to any one person, but to the concept. We defend it from all who would see it destroyed. Faith, loyalty, duty, nation. These are the things that those we honor today swore to uphold. . ."

Chuck Eberhardt, of the American Legion, summarized Holley's stalwart dedication to American ideals when he said: "Our little village has always answered our nation's call to arms and we have lost many of our young in defense of freedom."

"So Many Boys"

"I don't believe a day has passed since his death that I have not thought of him. He is permanently in my heart. I try to let him live through me as much as I can. I have tried to instill a sense of 'Uncle George' in my daughters. They know of his kindness, sense of humor, generosity and work ethic. So many boys were lost from such a small community. We knew them all. I would like to see them remembered for their living contributions, not only for their ultimate sacrifice."

~ *Patricia Fischer Nelson*

A Patriotic Community

"The community has always been very patriotic and will never forget the extreme sacrifices our servicemen made. Personally, I would like to see a memorial placed at the new flagpole in Hillside Cemetery listing the names of those who gave their lives."

~*Marsha DeFillips, Holley Town Historian & friend of the boys and their families*

The Memorial Day celebration included the dedication of the new Hillside Cemetery Memorial; a 30-foot spun aluminum flag pole, with a concrete, Pentagon-shaped base inlaid with five granite stones, bearing the insignia of each branch of the United States Military.

Eagle Scout candidate, Jacob Crandall, of Boy Scout Troop 59, worked to bring the memorial to fruition. John Crandall, Jacob's father, is a veteran of Desert Storm and Afghanistan forces. For many years, Crandall had been talking about creating such a memorial with Clarendon Town Historian, Melissa Lerlan, and now it is done.

Crandall explains that the black posts and chain surrounding the memorial flagpole designates it, "as a place to mourn and pay respect . . . and to remember those who have served."

It replaces the original flagpole erected by the family of Paul Mandracchia, one of the boys killed in Vietnam. It honored their son and all others who died serving their country. Sara Mandracchia, Paul's niece, received the United States flag lowered from the original monument. She said she was honored to receive the flag and called the new memorial, "beautiful".

A Noble But Futile Gesture

"At first I thought it was a noble gesture by our government to try to prevent the spread of Communism. As the war dragged on I changed my thinking and decided it was a futile gesture with too many young American men lost.

The way the returning soldiers were treated was terrible.

"After all these years, I still have a sense of heavy loss especially on Memorial Day, and his (David Case's) birthday, August 14. I think I feel it more strongly having been the closest sibling, but the whole family has lasting effects from this time.

"Personally, I knew every one of those boys that were lost. Several I counted as friends. It was a devastating loss for a town this size. Although the Holley memorial is small, their names that are on the memorial in Rochester are a very nice tribute to many of those who died."

~ *Bryan Case*

Four long decades after the Vietnam War, life goes on in Holley, just as it does in Vietnam.

Our ideals have not changed, despite immense human sacrifice and suffering brought on by the war. The simplest displays of freedom and an unwavering belief in the truths Americans hold dear, are perpetually seen in a place like Holley.

Do people in a place like Vietnam find comfort in *their* concept of freedom? It, too, is unchanging.

"Singing His Praise"

"I remember one time I had a friend over, unbeknownst to Ron. He came out of the bathroom in his underwear, spotted her and instead of getting embarrassed he marched straight through the living room to his bedroom saying 'hup...2...3...4'.

"He never seemed to take himself too seriously. He was all about enjoying life and helping others. I regret him not being around as each of our children was born. He would have held them on his lap and sang to them in that beautiful voice of his. Ron was always singing."

~ *Linda Johnson*

ACKNOWLEDGMENTS

Special thanks to the Bowen sisters, Debbie, Janet and Janice for being the first to respond to my rather cryptic letter which began this journey, and for allowing me to learn about your brother, "Howie". To Don Sisson, for helping me connect with your family and friends, and to appreciate your remarkable brother. To C. D. Smith, thank you for getting in touch and for sharing your stories about Ronnie and life in Vietnam. To Linda Sisson, many thanks for your heartfelt memories of Ronnie, (I know it wasn't easy). To Janice Stedman, thank you for your thoughts and feelings about Ron and about life in Holley. To Mary Anne Martin, thank you for your memories of your brother John. Special thanks to Patricia Nelson and your incredible photographs of George Jr. and especially the photo of the one legged chicken! To Robert Broekhuizen, many thanks for our phone conversations where I learned about your everlasting friendship with George Jr. and the races at Spencer and Lancaster! To Sharon Root, special thanks for allowing me into your beautiful home, and for sharing your photographs of Gary and your extended family. To Leslie, thank you for sharing your photographs and letters your brother Paul wrote from Vietnam and for introducing me to Aunt Rosa. And to Aunt Rosa, who taught me about Pop Louie's fish market in Canarsi! To Loren Preston, thank you for recounting your night in the Pentagon where you first learned about David's tragic death in Vietnam. To Darryl Cady who helped me find Bryan and then Susan and their great stories about David; the paper boy extraordinaire! To Duane and Marilee, for your wonderful photographs of Gary and where I learned for the first time about "the muck". To Marsha who allowed me access to letters, historical archives, newspaper articles and the wonderful images of Holley high school yearbooks. They were invaluable. To Lorraine, without whose help this book would not have been possible. And finally to the town of Holley, thank you for tolerating me these past several months.

APPENDIX A

The Pentagon Papers

The Report of the Office of the Secretary of Defense Vietnam Task Force, better known as the Pentagon Papers, was commissioned by the then Secretary of Defense, Robert McNamara, in 1967. The report is essentially a detailed summary of all the elements leading up to and during United States involvement in the Vietnam War. Deemed at the time, and for a considerable time thereafter, top secret and sensitive, pages of the report were first leaked in 1971. Most of that information was incomplete and inaccurately published.

In 2011, for the first time, the entirety of the report was released by the National Archives. More than 7,000 pages in length, the report is complete, without redaction, and as first presented in full to the then Secretary of Defense, Clark Clifford, in January of 1969.

The Papers are contained within six parts which consist of a total of 48 documents. Part I is called *Vietnam and the US*. It is a single document covering the years 1940-50. Part II is called *US Involvement in the Franco-Viet Minh War*. It is inclusive of the years 1950-54, and is also a single document. Part III is *The Geneva Accords*. Part IV is 26 distinct documents, divided into 10 subtitles. The document, overall, is called *Evolution of the War*. Part V is called

Justification of the War, and consists of Parts A and B, divided into 13 subtitles. Part VI is called *Settlement of the Conflict*. It consists of three subsections, and six subtitles in total.

The overall scope of the Papers is too immense to receive in this book the kind of attention it deserves. However, some comments and observations have been included to provide the type of in-the-moment and real-time insight that can be experienced simply by reading random selections.

We start with the fall of the French at Dien Bien Phu. Speaking on the contrast between the Vietnamese army and the French forces, and this as the French were departing Vietnam following their defeat at the hands of General Giap's Viet Minh, the report hints at the intensity inherent in the people of Vietnam, and what that intensity suggested were the United States to become involved militarily in that country.

> [The United States was] disturbed by the grim efficiency of the Viet Minh troops in their tennis shoes [in contrast to the] clanking armor of the French [who] had failed against the communist military-political-economic campaign (1954).

Reflecting on the Geneva Conventions, which were designed to bring a period of calm to Vietnam following the departure of the French, a time in which both the South and the North could reconcile their differences and unify, the Papers provide this telltale statement:

> The Geneva Settlement thus failed to provide lasting peace because it was, as US National Security Council papers of 1956 and 1958 aptly termed it, "only a truce." It failed to settle the role of the US or of the Saigon government, or, indeed, of France in Vietnam. It failed because it created two antagonist Vietnamese nations.

Referencing this so-called "period of calm", the report acknowledges "that the flow of arms into North Vietnam from China continued on a scale far in excess of 'replacement' needs."

It was clear to Washington that Ho Chi Minh and General Giap were strengthening the Viet Minh all the while, and that there was resentment for the South. Simply put, the lands south of the 17th Parallel were significantly more arable and the resources more plentiful.

The US reason for siding with the South was obvious. President Diem, at least on the surface, proposed a democratic government while Ho Chi Minh and the North had immediately adopted a Maoist approach. Washington's opinion of this development was summed up by this part of the report:

> On the broader level, the US decision to train the Vietnamese armed forces was viewed as necessary to preserve the independence and freedom of Vietnam south of the 17th parallel, an essential prerequisite to the containment of communism.

The report called the potential fall of Vietnam into the hands of communism as the Domino Effect. In other words, Washington believed that if Ho Chi Minh and the Viet Minh were allowed to overrun Saigon and displace President Diem that the entirety of the region, all of Indochina, would wind up in the hands of either Russia or China, thereby posing a worldwide threat to Democracy, the US, and the rest of the free world.

As far back as 1954, concerned with this very issue, Nixon, then Vice President, while addressing the American Society of Newspaper Editors, made it clear that there would be no negotiations with the Democratic Republic of Vietnam to divide the territory. He stated the following:

> It is hoped that the US will not have to send troops there, but if the government cannot avoid it, the administration must face up to the situation and dispatch forces.

From that point on, the US made massive investments in building South Vietnamese forces, all with the intent of countering the communist aim at overturning the 'legitimate' Government of

Vietnam, and with little success. Reflecting on this shortcoming, the report states:

> Unless the Vietnamese themselves show an inclination to make individual and collective sacrifices required to resist communism, which they have not done to date, no amount of external pressure and assistance can long delay complete Communist victory in South Vietnam.

The report makes it clear, however, that the US may have backed the wrong guy. President Diem's policies were not well-received by the population he governed. Their dissatisfaction was met with brutal tactics, including arrests, reeducation camps, executions, murder in the streets at the hands of Diem's police forces, and eventually what was known as 'regrouping' of the population. Peasants, especially, resented being forced from their ancestral lands and from family burial plots.

These conditions ultimately were responsible for the birth of the National Liberation Front (NLF), an organization of 'freedom fighters' that infiltrated the South and worked at recruiting members among the general population. The report describes the growth and influence of the NLF in the following words:

> By the time President Kennedy came to office in 1961, it was plain that support for the Saigon government among South Vietnam's peasants—90% of the population—was weak and waning. The Manifesto of the National Liberation Front, published in December 1960, trumpeted the existence of a revolutionary organization which could channel popular discontent into a political program. Increasingly Diem's government proved inept in dealing either through its public administration with the sources of popular discontent, or through its security apparatus with the Viet Cong. Diem's government and his party were by that time manifestly out of touch with the people, and into the gap between the government and the populace the Viet Cong

> had successfully driven. When and why this gap developed is crucial to an understanding of who the Viet Cong were, and to what extent they represented South as opposed to North Vietnamese interests.

Ultimately the NLF was to become the irregulars that made up the Viet Cong. The US Government, in its White Papers on Vietnam of 1961 and 1965, initially blamed the insurgency on aggression by Hanoi, holding that the Viet Cong were always tools of the DRV. It was later obligated to acknowledge that the two entities were separate and apart, at least at first.

In 1962, the US launched the Strategic Hamlet Program, the purpose of which was to develop support among the peasants for the central Vietnamese Government—the South. The idea was to clear an area of insurgents, hold it secure, and move on to the next area. Meanwhile, measures would be implemented to encourage the general population to more favorably view the government.

Unfortunately, the peasants viewed these measures as nothing more than "rural antagonisms" and an extension of the oppression they had already experienced under President Diem and his brother. Once the brothers had been assassinated, the leaders who took over distanced themselves from the program, and it collapsed leaving the insurgency to once again fill the void.

Following the death of President Diem, there was a period of optimism in which it appeared the Vietnamese Government was ready to listen to and heed US advice. However, by 1965, the South had suffered a series of military defeats at the hands of the VC. The US, fearing imminent collapse of the South, responded by increasing its involvement, including reinforcing the existing MACV teams with combat units. With this new level of involvement, the US role changed considerably:

> As the build-up of US combat forces reached a level permitting offensive forays against the VC (and North Vietnamese Army forces), there gradually evolved a division of responsibilities between US and Vietnamese forces in

> which the former were to concentrate on defeating the main forces of the VC/NVA and the latter were to give primary emphasis to the pacification program.

With the Tet Offensive in 1968, however, it became apparent to the US that assigning of a greater number of MACV advisors to assist the efforts of the South Vietnamese army was failing, as was the division of responsibility among US and South Vietnamese forces:

> This radical change in enemy tactics challenged the efficacy of the division of effort between US forces and RVNAF, shook US public support for the War, and marked the beginning of a new, uncharted phase in the history of US attempts to advise the government and armed forces of the Republic of Vietnam.

The remaining text of the Pentagon Papers detail each of the battles to follow, including Operation Rolling Thunder, the US invasion of DaNang, the different phases of the build-up of US Forces, force deployment, ground strategies, air war, and the eventual renewal in attempts to bring about pacification, including extensive justification for the war, and war in general, and the ultimate settlement of the conflict.

The Pentagon Papers can be fully accessed online at the following site:

http://www.archives.gov/research/pentagon-papers/

APPENDIX B

The Holley Marching Band

It was an event that I will never forget; in fact, I was standing next to a New York State Trooper when I heard him say he had "never seen anything like it." We were both standing in downtown Holley awaiting the Holley high school band from its record-breaking appearance at the New York State Fair high school marching band competition.

The school under the leadership of Ray Shahin had just won its third consecutive state band championship and fourth straight color guard championship. (It would eventually win a total of six state championships and was considered one of the best high school marching bands—ever).

For a community of its size, the three championships in a row was quite an accomplishment. Shahin insisted it's not one he can take sole credit for. Credit, he said goes to the people who helped him in drilling the band, to the many others in Holley who helped with cooperation of all kinds, and of course to the students themselves.

Music Heroes

Nevertheless, when the band returned from Syracuse thousands of our friends and relatives had waited up to three hours to greet Holley's conquering musical heroes.

By 10 o'clock, police estimated close to 1,000 people around the square; by 11 it was 2,000; by the time of the arrival of the band buses, escorted by the fire trucks of Holley, Clarendon, Kendall, and Brockport, a crowd estimated at 3,000 had gathered. No small feat as Holley's population was only 1,800! Incredibly, not only did it appear as everyone who lived in Holley had showed up but almost everyone in the county!

When the band lined up at the school and marched to the square to give us hometown folks a sample of what had won

The Holley high school marching band won a total of six state championships, the most of any school in the United States.

this community statewide honors once again, we let our musical heroes know by our reception how we felt about them.

What took place in the next few minutes would have amazed even the most blasé. Holley's people simply went wild with joy. Shouting, screaming, and pummeling one another, people dancing on benches, on the platform and all over the park. One rather staid Holley matron grabbed the astonished State Trooper I was standing next to and did an impromptu jig for a few seconds. Another usually reserved Holley citizen proceeded to demolish his hat by the simple expediency of beating his friend over the head with it.

Suddenly, the crowd grew momentarily quiet---as if the tumult had drained all possible noise. But a new sound filled the air. ---That of people sobbing---band members, color guard, mothers, and fathers---in a matter of minutes the once unrestrained crowd was now giving in to equally unrestrained tears.

It was a release from the terrible pressure and tension of competition and now expressed itself in the realization of victory and triumph. It was a happy contagion of sheer joy. After a good cry, we converged on the platform where Mr. Shahin was hoisted aloft and carried triumphantly through the square. Yes, as the State Trooper aptly put it: "I never saw anything like it."

~*Marsha DeFillips*

APPENDIX C

Ray Shahin

A native of Niagara Falls, Ray Shahin attended high school there and was appointed instrumental music director in Holley in 1953, the year he graduated from Fredonia State Teachers College where he majored in trumpet. While at Holley High School, he studied at the Eastman School of Music and received his Master's degree in music. He wrote all of the arrangements for the band and much of his music has been published. He started Holley's marching band that same year. Many other Orleans County high schools followed with their own marching bands as the result of Shahin's example.

Shahin's marching band won a total of six state championships, believed to be a record for any New York high school marching band and possibly in the country. Shahin also started adult musicals in Holley in 1961. He produced and arranged the music for such musicals as *The Sound of Music* and *Oklahoma*. He also was the director for the pit bands where he played his beloved trumpet. Additionally, Shahin wrote music for other high school bands as well as for many colleges. According to Holley historian Marsha Defillips, "the Holley band was legendary; he was a leader who touched so many lives."

Ray Shahin was the director of Holley's high school's marching band for all six of its state championships. He is described by many as a "great man" who devoted his life to teaching and leading students.

After 12 years at Holley, Shahin accepted a position as musical director for Bishop Kearney High School where he served from 1966 to 1983. In 2002 he was inducted into the Bishop Kearney Hall of Fame, making him perhaps one of the very few individuals to obtain that stature at two different schools.

Ray Shahin returned to Holley in 2000 to organize his former students to march and play in Holley's Centennial. One of his former students said after the event, "even at age 56 as I was preparing for the Holley band reunion, I had my wife give me frozen cucumber slices to reduce the swelling in my lips so that I could practice. My fear was that I would disappoint him!" Another of his former students said, "Ray was my Holley HS Band director, class of 1954. He was the major contributor to my mission to be a music teacher, conductor, clinician and music educator. What a great positive leader for creating sensitive musicianship and promoting self-esteem in all his students. He was truly a fabulous role model."

Ray Shahin passed away on July 24, 2012 at the age of 81.

Democrat & Chronicle, July 26, 2012

APPENDIX D

Notable Personalities

Dwight D. Eisenhower

Dwight D. Eisenhower followed Harry S. Truman as the President of the United States. Upon assuming office, he implemented his *New Look* program, a primary objective of which was to sustain the Cold War. With World War II still fresh from a global perspective, Eisenhower made no secret of his willingness to use nuclear weapons to deal with what he viewed as the growing threat of communism.

Starting with the Korean War, which Eisenhower believed had the potential to spread the Red Menace throughout East Asia, the president threatened to extend the war into China, who at the time was providing aid to North Korea. Russia, under new leadership following the death of Stalin, and having no wish to go to war, used its influence to convince China to lessen its role in the conflict, thereby effectively ending the war. Without formal resolution, the country was split in two, and a template for Vietnam created.

Eisenhower's disdain for communism remained as high as ever. Responding to overtures by Khrushchev, Stalin's successor, the President gave every impression of being willing to allow for a thaw in relations between the two countries. However, only days before a scheduled peace summit, Eisenhower authorized the use of U2 spy planes to fly over Russia for purposes of reconnaissance. At the summit, the Russian leader called out the President for doing so. Eisenhower, unaware that the U2 had been brought down by a Russian surface-to-air missile and the pilot captured, denied the accusation. Caught in the lie, the President, when asked for an apology by Khrushchev, refused. Khrushchev walked out of the summit and the Cold War escalated.

Eisenhower would later go on to extend his fight against communism into Central America, where US operatives manipulated the overthrow of a Marxist president, and to Cuba, authorizing the training of the rebel nationalists who were later captured during the Bay of Pigs invasion.

Ultimately, it was Eisenhower's obsession with the Red Menace and the potential spread of communism which brought the United States into Vietnam. As it became apparent that Ho Chi Minh and his Vietminh nationalist army was going to oust the French from Indochina, the President appealed to Congress for the necessary support to come to the aid of the French, which the US had been doing to that point only with money and weapons. It was during this particular press conference, in which Eisenhower made his infamous domino reference, stating:

> You have broader considerations that might follow what you would call the "falling domino" principle. You have a row of dominoes set up, you knock over the first one, and what will happen to the last one is the certainty that it will go over very quickly. So you could have a beginning of a disintegration that would have the most profound influences...Asia, after all, has already lost some 450 million of its peoples to the Communist dictatorship, and we simply can't afford greater losses.

Ultimately, Congress agreed to come to France's aid only if a multinational effort could be enjoined. No US ally stepped forth. Less than a month later, Dien Bien Phu fell to Ho Chi Minh.

The Geneva agreement, which was to follow, split Vietnam

in two. Not wanting to see Indochina fall into the hands of the communists, of which Ho Chi Minh was most definitely one, Eisenhower moved in to prop up the government of South Vietnam, and in the process set in motion the fall of the first domino in an altogether different row: the war in Vietnam.

Henry Kissinger

Following his election as the 37th president of the United States, Richard M. Nixon invited Henry Kissinger to become his National Security Advisor. Kissinger was born in Germany in 1923. He came to the United States in 1938, and was naturalized as a citizen in 1943. He served over-seas in WW II from 1943 to 1946.

Nixon chose Kissinger due to his belief that the two were of like mind with regard to Vietnam—that the US could exit the war with honor—as the Nixon campaign had promised. Kissinger, however, from the very beginning was of the belief that there was no way for the US to obtain a military victory, and that it would be impossible to reach an agreement with North Vietnam that didn't include giving the NLF—the Viet Cong—a significant role in the governing of South Vietnam.

Kissinger began negotiating secretly in Paris with the North Vietnamese, represented by Le Duc Tho, as early as 1968. The process was kept from Nguyen Van Thieu, the president of South Vietnam, as well as from the press here in the US and elsewhere. Little was accomplished early in the process due to Tho's insistence that the US cease bombing North Vietnam before any serious talks would take place, and his refusal to accede to US demands to have the NLF withdraw its Viet Cong guerrillas from South Vietnam before any bombing was brought to a halt. In addition, Le Duc Tho insisted on the establishment of a coalition government in South Vietnam which would replace President Thieu. Nixon, however, would not budge on this political issue, stating that he wasn't willing to politically displace a government the NLF had up to that point failed to overthrow militarily.

The two sides were at a stalemate that would last until 1972 when talks would again start to become meaningful.

In October of '72, Kissinger returned to Paris, following Nixon's national speech in which he said the US was willing to make some military concessions, thereby leaving the next move up to Hanoi. Le Duc Tho informed Kissinger that North Vietnam was willing to have Thieu remain in power in the South with the agreement that a unification process would be implemented in the near future, and he agreed to a unilateral cease-fire during which a prisoner exchange would take place.

Later that month, with the agreement in hand, Kissinger went to Saigon to meet with President Thieu. He outlined the key elements of the accord: There would be no coalition government; the US would rush financial aid to Saigon before the accord was official; South Vietnam would continue to receive full diplomatic and military support; the financial aid promised to North Vietnam to help build its physical infrastructure was dependent upon both Russia and China withdrawing their support—thereby isolating Hanoi; and, were Hanoi to renege on the agreement, President Nixon gave his word to immediately resume bombing of North Vietnam. Thieu listened without response.

When Kissinger and Thieu next met, Thieu was highly critical of the agreement. He was most distressed about the continued presence of NVA and NLF soldiers in the South, assuring Kissinger that this particular concession would doom his country and people. He accused Nixon of using the agreement as a way to appease voters here in the United States as to assure his re-election.

Following this second meeting, Kissinger informed Nixon as to Thieu's objections and the extensive changes in the agreement that he was requesting. Nixon, relying heavily on the advice of Al Haig, his Deputy Security Advisor, intimated that Kissinger should consider Thieu's concerns. Kissinger then left Saigon and returned to Paris where he reached out to Hanoi. He explained the impasse, expressed confidence that the agreement remained a good one, and asked for Hanoi's patience.

Hanoi responded by issuing a press release accusing the US of going-back on its promise—the agreement, and not having the backbone to stand up to Thieu. To compound matters, Hanoi released the agreement verbatim to the world.

Over the next two months, Kissinger remained in Paris negotiating with Le Duc Tho. Tho refused to allow any Saigon representatives to join the process, and he continued to seek greater concessions for the North. Nixon, his patience at an end with Tho's arrogance, responded by bombing Hanoi from the air, dropping more than a million tons of munitions onto the city. Within days of the aerial assault, the North requested a new start to the negotiations.

When Le Duc Tho came back to the negotiating table he was a humbler version of himself. He acquiesced to changes in the wording of the document to which he had prior objections, and he stopped making new demands. Regardless, the document that Kissinger brought back to President Thieu was inherently unchanged. To convince Thieu to agree to the peace accord, Nixon sent him letters of his own saying that the agreement satisfied the national interests of the United States and South Vietnam both, and that there was no better deal to be had. He closed by saying that the United States had given South Vietnam all it could in terms of blood.

The agreement was signed on January 27, 1973. Thieu's signature came with great reluctance. As a result of the Peace Accord, both Kissinger and Le Duc Tho were awarded the Nobel Prize. Tho immediately rejected the award; Kissinger was later to return it.

By May of '73, North Vietnam had already started to ignore those conditions of the treaty. It continued to accept aid from both Russia and China, and there was on-going terrorist activity in Saigon and throughout the South. Kissinger returned to Paris to try and convince Le Duc Tho to abide by the terms. However, by this time, Nixon and Watergate had weakened the office of the presidency. Congress was unwilling to supply any further economic aid to Saigon, or to prop up the government militarily. It didn't help any that Congress also wavered on providing the promised aid to North Vietnam, thereby removing any remaining incentive to Hanoi to comply.

In 1975, North Vietnam waged an all-out offensive against Saigon. The US Embassy came under fire, requiring extreme measures to evacuate US personnel. The city fell shortly thereafter. It was shortly after that Kissinger returned the Nobel to the committee.

Presently, Henry Kissinger is the chairman of Kissinger Associates, an international consulting firm, and continues to advise Washington on foreign affairs.

Ho Chi Minh

Ho Chi Minh, who was to change his name multiple times during his life, was born Nguyen Sinh Cung on May 19, 1890. He grew up in Hoang Tru in central Vietnam. His father, a teacher, was a member of the imperial court of the then French colony. His refusal to learn French—a requirement of the French government in Indochina—not only precluded him from teaching in any of the French run schools, but put him in opposition to those in charge. Eventually, he was to lose his position in the imperial court due to an alleged abuse of his power in which a man accused of a minor offense was caned to death.

No longer a man of influence, Ho's father was left to travel to nearby villages offering his services as a teacher. In the process, he cultivated an animosity towards French rule, which he held accountable for a social disparity resulting in the abject poverty he witnessed. That animosity was passed on to Ho Chi Minh, who even at a young age insisted on Vietnam's right to self-rule. Minh, himself, no longer capable of attending the French run school, left home, accepting a teaching position at a school in the south. Not long after, he decided he wanted to travel.

Now age 21, Minh—calling himself Nguyen Tat Thanh—

found work in the scullery aboard a French trading ship. For the next seven years, he traveled throughout much of Asia and Europe, and even perhaps as far as New York, where he claimed to have worked both in a Brooklyn hotel and for General Motors. He returned to Europe in 1913, first to London, and then moved to Paris in 1919, where he went under the name Nguyen Ai Quoc.

While in Paris, Minh became a representative for France's Socialist Party and was the founding member of the French Communist Party. During this period, he and other influential members of his group indirectly sought the support of Woodrow Wilson to free Vietnam from French rule and help establish a nationalist government. Failure to do so cemented Minh's communist values, and gave rise to his popularity back in Vietnam.

In 1923, the same year in which he was elected to the Committee of the Peasants' International Congress, Minh—under an assumed name—traveled to Moscow to join Comintern, Lenin's organization intent on spreading communist revolution throughout the world. After Moscow, Minh went to China where he joined up with young exiles from his own country and formed the Indo-Chinese Communist Party. It was these exiles who would later serve as the foundation for the Vietminh. In 1927, Minh was forced to leave China as a result of Chiang Kai-shek's rise to power. Chiang was an anti-communist.

Over the next decade, Minh moved about extensively, going from Moscow to Crimea, Paris to Thailand, with stops at Sweden and Italy, among other places, and eventually to Hong Kong via India. He was later arrested in Hong Kong by the British. The British, who at the time were being pressured by the French to have Minh extradited, declared him dead and released him. Minh, once again, returned to Russia. In 1938, he was allowed to return to China where he became an advisor for the Chinese Communist military. Twice during his ten-year exile, Minh contracted tuberculosis and required extended periods of convalescence.

In 1941, the Japanese invaded Indochina, taking military control of Vietnam and displacing the French. Ho Chi Minh took advantage of the unsettled environment to return to Vietnam. Once there, he organized the Viet Minh, personally taking charge of 10,000 elite fighters known as the *Men in Black*. His early actions against the Japanese were supported indirectly by the US Office of Strategic Services (OSS). The cooperation between the two was formalized in 1945 when Minh agreed to provide the US with information as to Japanese movements in exchange for training and munitions. It was during the first face-to-face meeting with the two sides that Minh was cured of a potentially deadly case of malaria by the OSS medic.

It was also in 1945 that the Japanese, fearing the advance of the US, and at the time co-occupying Indochina, used its military might to depose the French, ending more than 85 years of French rule. The Japanese, however, had no interest in local government. Emperor Bao Dai, supported by the Japanese, and then assumed responsibility, agreed at the same time to allow the Japanese military freedom of movement throughout Indochina.

During this brief period, there were a number of political parties active, most in the south. To the north, Ho Chi Minh was left unchecked to strengthen his position and influence. Using propaganda, Minh recruited and organized a large number of the peasants and farmers populating the countryside.

With the defeat of the Japanese in World War II, and their withdrawal from Vietnam, and before the French could again exert colonial claims, the nationalists, under Ho Chi Minh, took action. The Viet Minh seized control of Hanoi, obligating the then president, Tran Trong Kim, to resign, and using its own people to replace local government officials throughout the north. Ho Chi Minh offered the emperor an advisory position, which he accepted.

Minh did not have the same degree of success, or cooperation, in the southern part of the country. The political diversity was far greater than in the north, with none of the leaders of those different parties in any hurry to relinquish control to Minh. A different government was established in Saigon.

The on-going surrender of the Japanese following the end of

WW II only complicated matters. The country was divided by the Allies into two parts. While the Japanese troops to the north were left to surrender to the Chinese, Allied troops were sent to oversee the surrender to the south. Among the Allied troops were French soldiers. Taking advantage of the absence of a strong government in Saigon, the French reestablished its colonial claim and began operations anew. However, prohibited to go beyond the parallel by the Chinese, the French had no control over Hanoi or Ho Chi Minh.

Left to his own designs, Minh focused all of his efforts on eliminating any rivals to his government, thereby unifying the north under his command. In March of 1946, more as a delay tactic to give it time to reestablish its influence and military in Indochina, France agreed to Minh's petition to have Vietnam acknowledged as an independent state, but as part of the French Union. As part of the negotiations, the French agreed to restrict the number of troops it would send into the north, and to initiate a process to eventually unify all of Vietnam under a single government. Neither of which the French intended to honor.

Initially, Ho Chi Minh cooperated with the French, including killing those members of the nationalist movement opposed to communist rule. However, following a number of failed negotiations, late in 1946, Minh declared war against the French. With written messages similar to the one here, Minh rallied his people:

> Men and women, old and young, regardless of creeds, political parties, or nationalities, all the Vietnamese must stand up to fight the French colonialists to save the Fatherland. Those who have rifles will use their rifles. Those who have swords will use their swords. Those who have no swords will use their spades, hoes, and sticks. Everyone must endeavor to oppose the colonialists and save his country. (Ho Chi Minh Internet Archive, 2014)

Using mainly weapons left over from World War II and

primitive guerrilla warfare tactics, his Vietminh, supported by peasants and farmers, managed to destroy much of the French military infrastructure in the north. The strategy, though, took its toll, and exhausted, the Vietminh were forced to retreat.

Following multiple years of on-going warfare without significant advance, Ho Chi Minh decided to seek a truce. He organized a meeting with the French. During the negotiations, the French demanded that Minh hand over a number of Japanese military advisors who had been training his fighters. The French considered these Japanese war criminals. Minh refused. The negotiations ended there, and eight more years of fighting ensued. Finally, in 1954, Ho Chi Minh's troops defeated the French at Dien Bien Phu. The Geneva accord to follow opened the way to the US involvement in the Vietnam War.

Ho Chi Minh died of heart failure in 1969, and while he was still considered the leader of the Democratic Republic of Vietnam at that time, his role was primarily ceremonial. After the fall of Saigon in 1975, the city was renamed Ho Chi Minh City in his honor, and a memorial to his life-long efforts to establish Vietnam as an independent country.

Le Duc Tho

Le Duc Tho, the chief North Vietnam negotiator during the peace talks with Henry Kissinger, was born in 1911 in a middle class village in what was to become North Vietnam. Little is known about his early life, other than he served as a postal worker and had a major role in establishing the Indochinese Communist Party in 1929. In the 1930s, he was twice arrested and jailed for extended periods of time by the French for his involvement in protests against foreign rule. He was released in 1944 after serving five years.

Tho joined the Viet Minh during the French occupation. Serving as a chief deputy of the Communist Party situated in the southern part of the country, he quickly rose through the ranks during the French Indochina War to assume a senior position with the Viet Minh. In 1955, following the Geneva settlement Tho went north where he joined the Communist Politburo and gained the respect and admiration of Ho Chi Minh. Ultimately, Minh gave command of the Viet Cong to Tho.

When the Paris negotiations began towards the end of 1968, the chief North Vietnam representative was a communist leader by the name of Xuan Thuy. Members of the North Vietnam delegation, however, paid him little heed, ignoring his lead, and instead deferring to Le Duc Tho. By the beginning of 1969, most of the real negotiations were going on in secret between Tho and Kissinger. The two men would meet in a quiet, out of the way place in France, using diversions to slip away from journalists and lesser officials.

Later when referring to Tho, Kissinger identified him as a skillful but deceptive negotiator, and a man not readily willing to compromise. It was apparent to Kissinger that Tho made no distinction between a military and a political resolution, and would not bring back to Hanoi any agreement that did not provide for both.

Closer to the truth, however, is that Tho never had any intention of quitting the war in Vietnam until the country was unified under a single communist government. After reaching an agreement in principle with Kissinger in 1973, Tho returned to Vietnam, but was merely biding his time. As Nixon was withdrawing US troops and claiming victory, Tho still had 350,000 Viet Cong irregulars in South Vietnam. Over the next two years, he carefully planned the overthrow of President Thieu and the government in South Vietnam.

In 1985, Tho and Kissinger were again brought together, this time on ABC's Nightline hosted by Ted Koppel. Tho was in Ho Chi Minh City. Kissinger was here in New York. During the program, Tho made the statement that "[North Vietnam] wrested total victory" from the United States, and called the Vietnamization of the war a total failure. He then went on to thank the people of the United States "for their support and contributions to our present victory."

Kissinger responded by chiding the American media for demonstrating undue sympathy to Tho and North Vietnam, accusing Tho and Hanoi of violating the agreements of the Paris Peace Accord.

Tho would hold political influence in Vietnam until 1986 when a change in government obligated him to retire to private life. On October 13, 1990, following a long battle with cancer Tho passed away. He was 79.

Lyndon B. Johnson

Lyndon B. Johnson was serving as Vice President of the United States when John F. Kennedy was assassinated. On November 22, 1963, not quite three hours after the death of Kennedy, he became the country's 36th president.

Born in August of 1908, Johnson grew up in rural Texas. After graduating from college, he went to work as a teacher. In 1937, he was elected to the House of Representatives. He then served as a reservist in the Navy in World War II.

Initially stationed out of harm's way, Johnson was assigned by President Roosevelt to serve as part of a team commissioned to the South Pacific. While on a mission to bomb a Japanese target, the plane experienced trouble—which may or may not have been enemy related, and was required to abort. Regardless of the actual circumstances, Johnson was later awarded a Silver Star. Upon his return to civilian life, he was elected to the Senate, serving as both the Minority and Majority Leader.

Johnson became Kennedy's running mate after failing to win the Democratic nomination himself. After his defeat, Johnson actually came out against Kennedy's candidacy, campaigning openly with the hope of being named on a second ballot. That second ballot never materialized.

Despite Johnson's opposition, Kennedy realized that he was

trailing Nixon in the polls, and needed a means to appeal to voters in the south. He reached out to Johnson asking him to accept the nomination as Vice President. Johnson accepted.

A staunch defender of Democracy and opponent of Communism, Johnson, despite his preference to focus on issues here in the United States, continued in Kennedy's footsteps with regard to Eisenhower's *Domino Theory* and Vietnam. Expressing his concerns about the Red Menace taking hold in Indochina, Johnson said, "If we quit Vietnam, tomorrow we'll be fighting in Hawaii and next week we'll have to be fighting in San Francisco."

Nevertheless, Johnson was initially adamant about not sending ground troops into Vietnam, holding firm to the position that the South Vietnamese had to fight their own battle against the National Liberation Front (NLF). Later, he acknowledged the inevitability of doing so, but concerned with the negative perception of US involvement here at home, he refused to reconsider his position until after the 1964 election. It was an election he won by a landslide, defeating Barry Goldwater by more than 15 million votes.

Johnson's resolve, however, was tested in August of 1964, only months before the election. While doing reconnaissance in the Gulf of Tonkin, the commander of the *USS Maddox*, a naval destroyer, reported coming under attack by three North Vietnam torpedo boats. Despite the contradictory details provided, Johnson sought congressional endorsement to respond to the attacks with military force. Known as *The Gulf of Tonkin Resolution*, Congress gave the president the power to order military action against aggressors without first having a declaration of war. Johnson then proceeded to order air strikes against key North Vietnam installations along the coast and inland towards Hanoi.

With the '64 elections behind him, Johnson agreed to escalate US involvement in Vietnam. With US ground troops being limited to either an advisory role—embedded with South Vietnam troops, or stationed to defend US airfields, Johnson ordered an intensification of the bombing by air of North Vietnam—Operation Rolling Thunder. Ho Chi Minh responded by attacking the US airfields. Fearing the worst, the commander of the US advisors, General Westmoreland, requested reinforcements to bolster his defenses. Assuring the American people that it would be a short-term measure, Johnson ordered 3,500 Marines into Vietnam, making them the first US troops formally on the ground. The Tet Offensive would follow four years later.

On March 31, 1968, during a televised speech for that intended purpose, Johnson announced his decision not to run for re-election. Among his personal reasons, such as wishing to spend time with his family, getting to know his own grandchildren, and a concern for his health—both his father and grandfather died of heart failure at age 64, Johnson privately expressed regret over his role in the on-going war in Vietnam. Discussing the matter with confidants prior to his declaration, he expressed the challenge he was facing with the following words:

> *What if we're late in the campaign and I have to make a decision that might result in a peace settlement but will be politically risky…I want my hands free to do what's necessary to end this thing.*
>
> (Jones, 1988)

Presented with the opportunity later that year, and with hopes of taking the first steps towards lasting peace, Johnson called a halt to the bombing of North Vietnam. His actions failed to bring the end of the war, or to bring soldiers home. They did, however, give the then Vice President Hubert Humphrey a lift in the polls, making the election closer than predicted. Nixon won, nevertheless.

Lyndon B. Johnson died in January of 1973 while peace talks were going on under Nixon and Kissinger. Like his father and grandfather, he, too, suffered a fatal heart attack. He was 64 years of age.

Ngo Dinh Diem

In 1954, just prior to Ho Chi Minh's victory at Dien Bien Phu,

Bao Dai, the emperor of Vietnam, offered to Ngo Dinh Diem the position of Prime Minister of the new government of Vietnam. Though still under French control at the time, Bao Dai enjoyed some degree of independence. Diem accepted the position under the conditions that he has full control over the military and civil government, which he was granted.

Early in his leadership role, Diem faced significant opposition. Ultimately, his army defeated his enemies, providing him with the legitimacy he needed to move forward. In 1955, there were elections held in the south to decide between Bao Dai and Diem. Diem, relying on his brother and intense propaganda, had the process rigged. He won by a landslide, gaining significantly more votes than there were registered voters. Bao Dai was exiled, and Diem followed by declaring the upcoming unification election with North Vietnam null and void.

As the first President of South Vietnam, Diem immediately implemented programs to improve education—he established numerous universities, encouraged industry, built the infrastructure, reduced the nation's debt, and grew the economy, and stabilized currency and banking. His land reform policy, however, led to public dissension. In his attempt to redistribute the rural population in order to make better use of available land, he alienated peoples who refused to leave their ancestral homes. This alienation created opportunity for the Viet Cong—communists in the south—to gain sympathy, and provided the impetus for Diem's eventual assassination.

Richard M. Nixon

In the 1960 presidential election, Richard M. Nixon barely lost to John F. Kennedy. After the defeat, Nixon returned to civilian life and his law practice. With no real interest in getting back into politics, he nonetheless allowed himself to be talked into running for governor of California in 1962. Nixon again lost a close election, and this time stated publicly that he was done with politics.

He changed his mind in '67, when he declared his interest in again running for the presidency. At the time, the Republican Party had no strong candidate, and Nixon, believing the war in Vietnam had divided the Democrats—Johnson on one side, Robert Kennedy on the other, felt that he could win a close election. Capitalizing on the negativity building here in the States with regard to Vietnam, and Johnson's poor showing in the New Hampshire primary for the same reason, Nixon made the focus of his campaign the promise to end the war honorably, and bring US soldiers home.

Then the Tet Offensive happened. Johnson used its failure to press Hanoi on the issue of peace. Kissinger was sent back to Paris to meet with Tho.

Nixon, realizing that if a peace accord was reached his campaign would have nothing to stand on, allegedly derailed any possibility of a settlement. According to sources, Nixon had a source inside Washington providing him with information as to the on-going negotiations. Using that information, he then arranged for Anna Chennault—born in Beijing, the widow of the WW II commander of American operations in China, to use her personal ties with an influential South Vietnam Ambassador here in the States to get a message to President Thieu. That message was to reject any settlement coming out of Paris, with the promise that once elected; Nixon would obtain a more favorable one.

Johnson, who at the time had Thieu bugged, learned of Nixon's interference. He confronted Nixon with the knowledge. Nixon, however, aware of how Johnson obtained that knowledge, and that Johnson would not risk exposure to Thieu, denied it.

Regardless, Thieu rejected the conditions of the agreement, and Johnson made the decision not to run for re-election. Nixon beat Humphrey rather handily.

Shortly after assuming office, Nixon addressed the nation and borrowing from those who criticized the *Americanization* of the war under Johnson, introduced what he called his *Vietnamization* of the war. At the same time that he made his announcement,

Nixon informed the nation that 150,000 American soldiers were on their way home.

Interpreting the reduction of forces as an advantage, North Vietnam, ignoring the cease-fire that was in place, began a Tet-like assault throughout South Vietnam. The offensive was the first real test for Nixon's Vietnamization strategy. The South Vietnam soldiers were quickly overwhelmed, and had it not been for the support of US bombers, they would have been defeated. As it was, the Viet Cong were forced to retreat. That retreat was over the border, where the Viet Cong had long-established bases hidden in the Cambodian jungle.

Nixon, hoping to recruit Prince Sihanouk as an ally, had previously ignored recommendations by his generals to bomb Cambodia. Taking this most recent attack as a personal affront, he changed his mind. Keeping his decision secret for fear of public backlash, Nixon, with advice from Kissinger, ordered *Operation Menu*. The bombing began on May 18, 1969. The first wave was named Breakfast, and the waves to follow Lunch, Snack, Dinner, Supper, and Dessert.

By 1972, Nixon, advised by Kissinger that any further escalation would be futile, was looking for a way to fulfill his campaign promise. There were real signs that the Vietnamization process was working: The ARVN was having greater success; guerrilla fighters once fighting on the side of the NVA were integrating into the local villages; and, most of the Viet Cong had retreated north.

Nevertheless, Ton Duc Thang, having succeeded Ho Chi Minh, had something else in mind. Desperate to turn the tide of war back in favor of Hanoi, he launched *Operation Eastertide*. On March 30, General Giap sent twelve divisions backed by tanks and heavy artillery into South Vietnam.

Unprepared for the onslaught, most of the ARVN first encountered broke and ran. As the fighting wore on, however, ARVN troops, with assistance from continuous air support from American B52s, made a stand at the city of Hue, and then again and again in other cities.

Frustrated by their inability to advance, harassed endlessly by the B52s, and taking heavy casualties, the NVA retreated. It was by then early to mid-July.

It was in May, however, that Nixon came on television and told the American people that the only way to force North Vietnam to the peace table was to stop its ability to wage war. What was to follow were two major and extended bombing campaigns which reduced North Vietnam's infrastructure to rubble.

By the end of the summer, Hanoi returned to the peace talks. Nixon had his 'honorable' end to the war...and Watergate.

Robert McNamara

Robert McNamara was the Secretary of Defense who served under both John F. Kennedy and Lyndon B. Johnson. A statistical analysis wizard with both a military—albeit desk job—and business background, he was ultimately to become the architect of the war in Vietnam.

McNamara was born in 1916, the son of an Irish Immigrant who came to the States as a result of the Great Hunger which plagued Ireland in the late 1840s. Raised in California, he graduated from Berkley with a degree in economics and math. He went on to earn a graduate degree from Harvard.

While at Harvard, McNamara taught an analytics class to officers from the US Army Air Forces (USAAF). Inspired, he himself joined the USAAF in 1943. He was assigned to the Office of Statistical Control, where his primary responsibility was to crunch numbers relative to efficiency. Ultimately, he devised a schedule wherein B52 bombers could serve a dual purpose, not only bombing but delivering fuel and cargo.

Once out of the military, McNamara and a group of fellow veterans formed part of a team—dubbed the Whiz Kids—that was hired by Henry Ford II to help turn around his floundering car manufacturer. McNamara was credited with the concepts behind the Ford Falcon and the Lincoln Continental, smaller, cheaper car models based on safety and cost efficiency, and which gave the consumer a choice over older and less popular Ford models. Due to his ingenuity and success, McNamara was named president of the Ford Motor Company, the first ever not of the Ford family.

Hardly more than a month or two in his new position, McNamara was approached by Kennedy to become the Secretary of Defense. Kennedy had originally offered the position to Robert Lovett, a former Secretary of State. Lovett, who had been in the private sector at the time, declined, citing health reasons. It was he who suggested McNamara. McNamara accepted, though he recalled saying at the time that he could barely tell a nuclear warhead from a station wagon.

As the Secretary of Defense, McNamara's first task was to investigate whether Russia's nuclear power was greater than that of the US, as suggested by the Eisenhower administration. Using US spy satellites, he determined that the US arsenal and ability to deliver missiles was far greater than that of Russia, attributing the misinformation to guess work and a lack of real data.

It was also McNamara who convinced Kennedy and Johnson that a nuclear war could not be won—Eisenhower was an advocate of nuclear attacks, and instead suggested the concept of limited or strategic warfare in which such weapons would not be used. It was McNamara's counterinsurgency ideas which led to the creation of US Special Forces designed to deal with guerrilla and non-conventional warfare.

McNamara was also assigned by Kennedy the task of determining a military strategy for overthrowing Castro following the Bay of Pigs disaster. He calculated it would take approximately sixty thousand ground troops. However, McNamara also stated "the government should never start anything unless it could be finished…or was willing to face the consequence of failure." Kennedy chose not to follow through with the plan.

In 1962, Russian leader Nikita Khrushchev, in response to the US positioning of nuclear warheads in Turkey, sent similar weapons to Cuba. Washington's initial response was to consider an all-out military strike on Cuba. McNamara advised Kennedy that such an action would in all likelihood escalate into a war with Russia—and the use of nuclear weapons. Instead, he suggested removing the nuclear missiles from Turkey, and then asking Khrushchev to do the same. The tactic worked, bringing an end to the Cuban Missile Crisis.

In April of that same year, McNamara made his first visit to South Vietnam. At the time, US involvement was limited to financial support of the South Vietnamese government, and the covert assistance of military advisors—small groups of ground troops whose purpose was to train the South Vietnamese army, but not to engage the enemy. Following his return to the States, McNamara declared US efforts a success. Using statistical analysis, he predicted the war would end favorably in three to four years.

Nevertheless, it was partially through McNamara's own actions in response to the supposed attack on the *USS Maddox* in the Gulf of Tonkin that the war would stretch on for more than ten years. Depending on perspective, McNamara either chose to present unverified, raw intelligence to President Johnson, or he made a calculated decision to withhold from Johnson messages forwarded by Captain John Herrick, commander of a second ship there in the Gulf, suggesting there was no attack and requesting a delay in military response pending confirmation.

Based on the intelligence provided to him by McNamara, and his strong encouragement, Johnson ordered the bombing of key North Vietnam installations along the coast. He then halted those bombing raids only days later when he learned that he might not have been accurately informed. According to official documents, McNamara twice more over the next weeks came to Johnson with reports of similar incidents. Johnson refused to resume bombing.

However, in January of '65, McNamara and McGeorge Bundy, National Security Advisor, convinced that Johnson was willing to lose in Vietnam, co-wrote a letter to the president stating that his continued passivity would lead to a national humiliation which would fall on his shoulders. Johnson responded by launching *Operation Rolling Thunder*.

It was in February '66, after the US had dropped hundreds of thousands of tons of munitions on North Vietnam at a cost of over $460 million—yet failed to stop the flow of NVA and weapons into the South—that McNamara acknowledged that "...no amount of bombing can end the war," concluding, in fact, that nothing the US could do would defeat the North Vietnamese.

It was at this time, and with a change in attitude towards the war, that McNamara directed his team to start assembling all available documentation related to the war. These documents would become *The Pentagon Papers*.

In May of '67, McNamara informed Johnson that he thought the only logical action was to negotiate a truce with North Vietnam. He cited the unpopularity of the war here in the US, its financial cost, and the unjust consequences suffered by non-military combatants throughout Vietnam. McNamara concluded his correspondence using the following words: "All want the war ended and expect their president to end it. Successfully. Or else."

Johnson interpreted these final words as a veiled threat, assuming that McNamara had already made up his mind to run as Vice President on the Robert Kennedy ticket against Johnson for the '68 elections. The president responded by indirectly removing McNamara from his post.

Years later, McNamara would say with regard to the Vietnam War, "What went wrong was a basic misunderstanding or misevaluation of the threat to our security represented by the North Vietnamese...I am certain we exaggerated the threat."

Robert S. McNamara, the architect of the war in Vietnam, died on July 6, 2009. He was 93.

Vo Nguyen Giap

Vo Nguyen Giap (pronunciation *vo nwin zhap*) was considered by his peers to be a military genius, along the line of MacArthur and Rommel. Born in 1911 in a peasant village in the southern extreme of what was to become North Vietnam, he was raised by his father to be an extreme nationalist with disdain for the French occupation. While attending a French sponsored high school, Giap was expelled for organizing a student strike against the French. He would go on to earn a degree in political economy and law from the University of Hanoi. Following his graduation, he took a position teaching. He was arrested in 1930 for again leading student strikes against the occupation. Upon his release, Giap officially became a member of the communist party.

In 1940, Giap, fearing further persecution by the French authorities—communism had been recently outlawed, fled to China. It was here that he first aligned himself with Ho Chi Minh. As a member of Ho's Viet Minh, he returned to Indochina during the latter part of WWII to engage in guerilla warfare against the Japanese.

With the defeat of the Japanese at the hands of the Allies, there was a gap in which Indochina was neither occupied or under foreign rule. Ho Chi Minh took advantage of this gap and declared the Democratic Republic of Vietnam an independent state. He then appointed Giap his interior minister. Despite the fact that Giap had no formal military training, his title was changed to commander of the Viet Minh military when the French returned and refused to recognize Ho's government.

Giap quickly learned that his men were no match for the mechanized might of the French in a traditional war. He responded by retreating with the Viet Minh into the hills and valleys of the deep jungle, leaving the major cities and towns to the occupation. Hoping to draw the French away from their strongholds, Giap raided over the border into Laos. His plan was to bring the French troops into terrain where their armored vehicles and tanks would do them no good, and where his guerilla fighters would have the advantage.

Navarre, however, instead countered by gathering his troops into the valley at Dien Bien Phu, thereby forcing Giap to come to him. Giap came, but not in the way Navarre had anticipated, and definitely not with the results the French commander had hoped for.

Following the Geneva peace accords, Ho Chi Minh named Giap the minister of defense and commander-in-chief of the NVA. A decade later, Giap brought against the Americans and South Vietnamese a war based on terrorism and guerrilla warfare, strategies he adapted from his studies of Mao Zedong.

As a general, Giap took full advantage of his fighters' willingness to die in defense of their ancestral lands. With regards to the millions of NVA and Viet Cong casualties, Giap stated, "The life or death of…tens of thousands of human beings, even our compatriots, means little."

Giap was the architect of the Tet Offensive. His intent was to replicate his victory at Dien Bien Phu, and at the same time bring the horror and destruction of the war into the American home. More than just a soldier, Giap understood the psychology of war, and the impact television and the media could have when the average American saw that the imminent victory of which they had been assured was at the best an optimistic estimate, and at the worst, a calculated misrepresentation.

Ultimately, the Tet Offensive failed, not because Giap's plan was a poor one, but because the Viet Cong irregulars lacked the discipline and coordination to execute the terrorist attacks throughout the cities in an effective manner, acting before regular NVA were in place to provide support. The uprisings were put down relatively easily, and mostly by ARVN.

With his two-pronged approach, Giap had hoped to draw US forces away from Khe Sanh, leaving the base under-defended. The success of the ARVN, however, allowed the US to fortify the base. Despite being extremely out-numbered, the US troops at Khe Sanh were well-entrenched, effectively resupplied by air drops, and held the high ground. Giap's NVA were eventually defeated.

Although the Tet Offensive was an abject failure by the North in military terms, Giap was satisfied with the message it sent to the people in the States: The war in Vietnam could not be won; the

NVA and the Viet Cong would fight to the death.

Nevertheless, the failure of the Tet Offensive did have its tactical consequences: The NVA was effectively weakened, the Viet Cong irregulars were forced into hiding, and Nixon's Vietnamization was given the time to take hold. With Hanoi seeing its influence south of the parallel slipping, Giap devised a military plan based on more conventional warfare. The Eastertide Operation would be his last as the mastermind of the Hanoi effort. Criticized for the huge number of casualties the NVA took at the hands of US B52 bombers, and the failure to hold any of the gains made at the onset of the operation, Giap was replaced by President Thang as commander-in-chief.

Giap, however, held on to his title as minister of defense. In that position, he oversaw both the 1975 overthrow of the South Vietnam government in Saigon, and the overthrow of the Khmer Rouge in Cambodia. Unfortunately, the Chinese, perhaps concerned that Hanoi was getting too confident and in need of a reminder as to who the real power in East Asia was, attacked along the border of North Vietnam. Convinced that Giap's better days were behind him, Thang's administration removed him from office. Giap, instead, was appointed the prime minister for science and education. He held that position until 1991 when another change in government led to his retirement from public service.

Giap died in October of 2013. He was believed to be 102 years of age.

William Westmoreland

To get an impression of General William Westmoreland one need only consider the following: It was said that when he met one-on-one in briefing meetings with one of his subordinates or advisors, while that particular individual was delivering the intended information, Westmoreland would occupy himself by autographing piles of his own photos.

Born in South Carolina in 1914 into a family with a long and distinguished military background, Westmoreland was educated at both the Citadel and then at West Point. His first combat assignment came in WWII where he was a battalion commander. Following his transfer to the European theater, he became a division chief of staff. By 1952, Westmoreland had attained the rank of lieutenant colonel, commanding a combat regiment in Korea. He returned to West Point in 1960 to become the school's superintendent.

In 1963, Westmoreland was sent to Vietnam to coordinate the military advisors—MACV—who were assisting the South Vietnamese against the NVA and the Viet Cong. By 1964, these men numbered 16,000. Following the Gulf of Tonkin incident—and Johnson's response, Westmoreland was put in charge of MACV.

As the US response in Vietnam escalated, President Johnson gave Westmoreland complete command of all military operations. A traditionalist, the general preferred a search and destroy approach in which hundreds of US ground troops at a time were sent into the jungle to draw out the NVA and Viet Cong—when and if they would cooperate—where they would be no match for superior force and weapons. The general believed the war would be won by attrition. In other words, his aim was to kill so many Viet Cong—a force he estimated at no more than 300,000—that there would be no one left to fight.

While Westmoreland's tactics did result in a high number of enemy casualties, his critics tended to believe he overinflated those numbers, while at the same time underestimating both the number of Viet Cong, and how quickly those numbers were being replenished.

Overall, the consensus of his detractors was that Westmoreland either didn't understand or refused to accept that the real war was taking place in the villages where the Viet Cong were hiding in plain sight among the locals, using intimidation to avoid detection, and rendering useless the weaponry of conventional war.

When called on his strategy by Washington—which included

ordering more than 535,000 US troops into Vietnam, Westmoreland pointed to early victories as evidence of its effectiveness. He then went on to ensure President Johnson and the American people that victory was within reach, intimating that the Viet Cong, in terms of numbers, had been severely reduced.

It was this overly optimistic assessment by Westmoreland that led to accusations that he was both surprised by and unprepared for the Tet Offensive. Despite the fact that he ultimately handed Hanoi and Giap a costly defeat, the extent of the attack provided indisputable evidence—both to Washington and the American people—that Westmoreland, whether out of arrogance or for some calculated purpose, underestimated both the size and tenacity of his enemy.

Stung by the criticism, Westmoreland, nonetheless, insisted on sticking to his guns. He immediately requested Johnson authorize the sending of 200,000 additional US troops to Vietnam. Johnson, well aware of the growing disenchantment with the war in the States, delayed his initial response. Two months later, Westmoreland was called back from Vietnam, and replaced by General Creighton Adams. Adams, at the time, was serving as the MACV commander, a role which included command of both the Marine and Army troops fighting in the north. Ironically, Adams had been promoted to that position by Westmoreland himself due to the general's lack of confidence in the military professionalism and efficiency of those two branches.

Following his return to Washington, Westmoreland was named Army Chief of Staff. Ultimately, he had a role early on in Nixon's plan for transitioning US troops out of Vietnam. As part of the process, he advocated for an all-volunteer United States Army, and even went so far as to modify some elements of regimentation to make serving more appealing to young men. It also fell to Westmoreland to investigate the events of the My Lai Massacre. The results of that investigation, however, were not made public until after Westmoreland resigned from office in 1972.

NOTES

CHAPTER ONE

1. en.wikipedia.org/ wiki/ Mineral_lick
2. en.wikipedia.org/ wiki/ Myron_Holley
3. Young, Holice B., Transcriber. *The Pioneer History of Orleans County, NY.*

CHAPTER TWO

1. www.english.illinois.edu/ maps/ vietnam/ antiwar.ht ml
2. www.lonelyplanet.com/ vietnam/ history
3. asia.isp.msu.edu/ wbwoa/ southeast_asia/ vietnam/ history.htm
4. alphahistory.com/ vietnamwar/ vietnam-before-french-colonisation
5. www.digitalhistory.uh.edu/ teachers/ lesson_plans/ pdfs/ unit12_1.pdf
6. en.wikipedia.org/ wiki/ Communism *In political and social sciences, Communism is a social, political, and economic ideology/ movement whose ultimate goal is the establishment of the communist society; which is a socio-economic order structured upon the common ownership of the means of production and the absence of social classes, money, and the state.
7. en.wikipedia.org/ wiki/ Ho_Chi_Minh
8. en.wikipedia.org/ wiki/ Guerrilla_warfare Guerrilla warfare is a form of irregular warfare in which a small group of combatants such as paramilitary personnel, armed civilians, or irregulars use military tactics including ambushes, sabotage, raids, petty warfare, hit-and-run tactics, and mobility to fight a larger and less-mobile traditional military.

CHAPTER THREE

1. en.wikipedia.org/ wiki/ Long_B%C3%ACnh_ward
2. www.medicinenet.com/ hepatitis_a/ article.htm

3. www.who.int/water_sanitation_health/diseases/leptospirosis/en/

INTERVIEWS:
Ann Martin, April 11, 2016, April 22, 2016

CHAPTER FOUR

1. 2012. Farewell, Isabelle. Retrieved on May 27, 2016 from: hystoricus.wordpress.com/tag/the-battle-of-dien-bien-phu/
2. Noah, Joe. 1995. Secret Flight from Ashiya to Hanoi. The Green Hornets, 61st TCS and ALS Squadron. Retrieved on May 27, 2016 from: 61tcs.org/stories.htm

CHAPTER FIVE

INTERVIEWS:
Loren Preston, 6/11/2016
Darryl Cady, 7/29, 2016
Bryan Case, 7/14/2016, 7/30, 2016, 8/17, 2016
Susan (Case) Hill, 8/2/2016

CHAPTER SIX

1. David Kaiser, Thomas Schwartz, Eric Bergerud. 2003. *Was Kennedy Behind the Assassination of Diem?* History News Network. Retrieved on May 27, 2016 from: historynewsnetwork.org/article/1717
2. Post Editorial Board. 2013. The other assassination of 1963. The New York Post. Retrieved on May 27, 2016 from: nypost.com/2013/11/16/the-other-assassination-of-1963/
3. John Prados. 2003. JKF and the Diem Coup. The National Security Archive. Retrieved on May 27, 2016 from nsarchive.gwu.edu/NSAEBB/NSAEBB101/

CHAPTER SEVEN

INTERVIEWS:
Donald Sisson, 3/23/2016, 5/9/2016, 6/16/2016, 8/11/2016
Charles D. Smith, 3/30/2016, 6/19/2016, 8/3/2016
Paula Ochs, 3/12/2016
Duane Good, 4/1/2016
Linda (Sisson) Johnson, 6/9/2016, 7/28/2016, 8/18/2016
Janice Stedman, 7/7/2016, 8/9/ 2016

CHAPTER EIGHT

1. Pat Peterson. 2008. The Truth about Tonkin. Naval History Magazine, Vol 22, No 1. Retrieved on May 29, 2016 from: www.usni.org/magazines/navalhistory/2008-02/truth-about-tonkin
2. Gareth Porter. 2013. The Real Tonkin Gulf Deception Wasn't by Lyndon Johnson. Truthout. Retrieved on May 29, 2016 from: www.truth-out.org/news/item/25377-the-real-tonkin-gulf-deception-wasnt-by-lyndon-johnson

CHAPTER NINE

1. scienceline.org/2006/07/ask-cosier-skunk/
2. www.motherearthnews.com/homesteading-and-livestock/how-to-butcher-a-homestead-raised-hog-zmaz82sozgoe.aspx

INTERVIEWS
Debbie (Bowen) Roe, 3/18/2016, 3/28/2016
Jane (Bowen) Robinson, 4/16/2016, 5/13/2016
Janet (Bowen) Dennis, 4/16/2016, 6/2/2016

CHAPTER TEN

1. Walter Cronkite. 1968. We Are Mired in Stalemate. Retrieved June 2, 2016 from: facultystaff.richmond.edu/~ebolt/history398/Cronkite_1968.html
2. Alan Woods. 2008. The Tet Offensive: the turning point in the Vietnam War. In Defense of Marxism. Retrieved June 2, 2016 from: www.marxist.com/tet-offensive-part-one.htm
3. Also: Tet Offensive. Vets with a Mission. Retrieved June 3, 2016 from: www.vwam.com/vets/tet/tet.html

CHAPTER ELEVEN

1. www.jrwatkins.com/timeline#
2. Signor, Isaac S. Landmarks of Orleans County, New York. D. Mason & Company, Syracuse, N.Y. 1894. Chapter 5
3. Gibson, Irene M. History of the First Methodist Church, Holley, New York (1869-1966).
4. en.wikipedia.org/wiki/Holley_Village_Historic_District
5. Records of the Military Assistance Command Vietnam: Part 1. The War in Vietnam 1954-1973, MACV Historical Office Collection.

INTERVIEWS:
Sharon Root, March 30, 2016, April 13, 2016, May 28, 2016, July 12, 2016

EMAILS:

Fred Ramsey, June 11, 2016

CHAPTER TWELVE

1. Introduction: My Lai. Thirteen. American Experience. Retrieved June 7, 2016 from: www.pbs.org/wgbh/americanexperience/features/introduction/mylai/
2. 2005. The My Lai Massacre. Thirteen. American Experience. Retrieved June 7, 2016 from: www.pbs.org/wgbh/amex/vietnam/trenches/my_lai.html
3. 2016. My Lai Massacre. Explorations: The Vietnam War as History. Digital History. Retrieved June 7, 2016 from: www.digitalhistory.uh.edu/active_learning/explorations/vietnam/vietnam_mylai.cfm

CHAPTER THIRTEEN

1. Genter, Betty Sherwood. *Growing Up On a Muckland Farm* (Self Published, 2003)
2. en.wikipedia.org/wiki/Cooper_(profession)
3. www.madehow.com/Volume-4/Bowling-Pin.html
4. www.amfbowling.com.au/alley-chat/bowling/how-bowling-pins-are-made

INTERVIEWS:
Duane Stymus, March 23, 2016, April 19, 2016, June 17, 2017
Marilee Lee (Stymus) Press, April 11, 2016, June 19, 2016, August 3, 2016

CHAPTER FOURTEEN

1. Tyler Owen and Ben Kiernan. 2007. Bombs Over Cambodia: New Light on US Air War. The Asia-Pacific Journal. Retrieved June 5, 2016 from: apjjf.org/-Taylor-Owen/2420/article.html
2. Jerry M. Lewis and Thomas R. Hensley. 1998. The May 4 Shootings at Kent State University: The Search for Historical Accuracy. The Ohio Council for the Social Studies Review. Vol 34, no 1. Retrieved June 5, 2016 from: dept.kent.edu/sociology/lewis/lewihen.htm

CHAPTER FIFTEEN

INTERVIEWS:
Robert Broekhuizen, April 8, 2016, April 22, 2016
Patricia Nelson, April 3, 2016, April 11, 2016, April 21, 2016
Gary Kent, April 2, 2016

EMAILS:
Patricia Nelson, April 5, 9, 23, 25, 2016

LETTERS:
Leonard Kasper
1.www.stanleytools.com/products/automotive-tools
2.www.mactools.com/en-us
3.www.timeout.com/newyork/events-festivals/macys-thanksgiving-day-parade

CHAPTER SIXTEEN

1. Cease-Fire. The 1st Battalion 50th Infantry Association Website. Retrieved June 13, 2016 from: www.ichiban1.org/html/history/1969_1973_vietnamization/17_vietnam_cease_fire_1972_1973.htm
2. The Pentagon Papers. Retrieved on June 13, 2016 from: www.archives.gov/research/pentagon-papers/
3. Tucker, Spencer, ed. (1998). *Encyclopedia of the Vietnam War: A Political, Social, and Military History. Volume Two.* Santa Barbara

CHAPTER SEVENTEEN

1. www.everyculture.com/multi/Pa-Sp/Sicilian-Ame ricans.html
2. www.directferries.com/palermo_napoli_ferry.htm
3. en.wikipedia.org/wiki/Statue_of_Liberty
4. www.italiangenealogy.com/forum/emigration/7347
5. presentations/immigration/italian3.html
6. www.iwm.org.uk/history/what-life-was-like-in-britain-during-the-second-world-war

INTERVIEWS:
Leslie Mandracchia, May 22, 2016, June, 16, 2016, June 30, 2016
Rosa Alberti May 27, 2016
Vietnam Message Board:
Todd Defrank, May 1, 2016

APPENDIX D

WESTMORELAND

Westmoreland died in July of 2005. Despite his efforts to the contrary, he failed to fully distance himself from the reputation of being the man who lost the Vietnam War.

William Westmoreland, Biography. Retrieved from: www.biography.com/people/william-westmoreland-9528510

Hickman, Kennedy. September 2015. Vietnam War: General William Westmoreland. Retrieved from: militaryhistory.about.com/od/1900s/p/westmoreland.htm

Thompson, Mark. September 2011. The General Who Lost Vietnam. Retrieved from: nation.time.com/2011/09/30/the-general-who-lost-vietnam/

GIAP

Gregory, Joseph R. October 4, 2013. Gen. Vo Nguyen Giap, Who Ousted US from Vietnam, Is Dead. *The New York Times*. Retrieved from: www.nytimes.com/2013/10/05/world/asia/gen-vo-nguyen-giap-dies.html?_r=0

Hickman, Kennedy. August 2016. Vietnam War: Vo Nguyen Giap. Retrieved from: militaryhistory.about.com/od/army/p/giap.htm

MCNAMARA

Porter, Gareth. August 5, 2014. Robert S. McNamara and the Real Tonkin Gulf Deception. Retrieved from: www.counterpunch.org/2014/08/05/robert-s-mcnamara-and-the-real-tonkin-gulf-deception/

Weiner, Tim. July 6, 2009. Robert S. McNamara, Architect of a Futile War, Dies at 93. Retrieved from: www.nytimes.com/2009/07/07/us/07mcnamara.html?pagewanted=all&_r=0

NIXON

James K. Moore. September 2006. North Vietnamese Army's 1972 Eastertide Offensive. Retrieved from: www.historynet.com/north-vietnamese-armys-1972-eastertide-offensive.htm

The Secret Bombing of Cambodia, Nixon's Fatal Decision. Retrieved from: sites.google.com/site/thesecretbombingofcambodia/introduction

Schultz, Colin. March 2013. Nixon Prolonged Vietnam War for Political Gain—And Johnson Knew About It, Newly Unclassified Tapes Suggest. Retrieved from: www.smithsonianmag.com/smart-news/nixon-prolonged-vietnam-war-for-political-gainand-johnson-knew-about-it-newly-unclassified-tapes-suggest-3595441/?no-ist

JOHNSON

C N Trueman. "Lyndon Johnson and Vietnam" historylearningsite.co.uk. The History Learning Site. 27 March 2015. 19 July 2016.

Frank Freidel and Hugh Sidey. 2016. The Presidents of the United States of America. Retrieved from: www.whitehouse.gov/1600/presidents/lyndonbjohnson

James R. Jones. 1988. Behind L.B.J.'s Decision Not to Run in '68. *The New York Times*. Retrieved from: www.nytimes.com/1988/04/16/opinion/behind-lbj-s-decision-not-to-run-in-68.html

KISSINGER

Dowd, Maureen. May 1, 1985. KISSINGER AND LE DUC THO MEET AGAIN, AND BITTERNESS SHOWS. *The New York Times*. Retrieved from: www.nytimes.com/1985/05/01/world/kissinger-and-le-duc-tho-meet-again-and-bitterness-shows.html

Page, Eric. October 1990. Le Duc Tho, Top Hanoi Aide, Dies at 79. *The New York Times*. Retrieved from: www.nytimes.com/1990/10/14/obituaries/le-duc-tho-top-hanoi-aide-dies-at-79.html?pagewanted=all

HO CHI MINH

Ho Chi Minh (1890-1969). Retrieved from www.bbc.co.uk/history/historic_figures/ho_chi_minh.shtml

Biography of Ho Chi Minh. Retrieved from www.marxists.org/reference/archive/ho-chi-minh/biography.htm (There's a link on this page that goes to a collection of documents.)

Chris Sibilla. A Peace that Couldn't Last—Negotiating the Paris Accords on Vietnam. Retrieved from: adst.org/2016/01/a-peace-that-couldnt-last-negotiating-the-paris-accords-on-vietnam/

EISENHOWER

The Row of Dominoes, Dwight D. Eisenhower, Presidential Press Conference, April 7, 1954. Retrieved from: www.vietnamwar.net/Eisenhower-2.htm

Miller Center of Public Affairs, University of Virginia. "Dwight D. Eisenhower: Foreign Affairs." Accessed August 12, 2016. millercenter.

BIBLIOGRAPHY

Holley

Defillips, Herlan. *Hillside Cemetery-125 Years* (Isselhard, 1992)

Defillips, Marsha. *Pictorial History of the Square-Holley, New York.* (Raymond Santore, 1991)

Genter, Betty Sherwood. *Growing Up On a Muckland Farm* (Self Published, 2003)

Pratt, Howard J. *Memories of Life on the Ridge.* (Orleans County Historical Society, 1978)

Reisem, Richeard O. *Myron Holley: Canal Builder/Abolitionist/Unsung Hero.* (Friends of Mount Hope Cemetery, 2013)

Vanderlaan, Stanley. *Growing Up and Growing Old on the County House Road.* (Self Published, 2005)

Vietnam

Arnold, James R. *The First Domino: Eisenhower, the Military, and America's Intervention in Vietnam.* (William Morrow & Co., 1991)

Baker, Mark. Nam. *The Vietnam War in the Words of the Men and Women Who Fought There* (William Morrow and Company, INC. 1981)

Bao, Ninh. *The Sorrow of War.* (Pantheon Books, 1990)

Dallek, Robert. Nixon and Kissinger: Partners in Power, (Harper Collins, 2007)

Ellsberg, Daniel. *The Pentagon Papers: United States-Vietnam Relations, 1945-1967: A Study Prepared by the Department of Defense.* Originally released by; *The New York Times,* 1971.

Fitzgerald, Frances, *Fire in the Lake: The Vietnamese and the Americans in Vietnam.* (Little & Brown Co., 1992)

Halberstam, David. *The Best and the Brightest.* (Random House, 1972)

Hammer, Ellen, J. *A Death in November: America in Vietnam 1963* (Oxford University Press, 1987)

Laurence, John. *The Cat from Hue.* (The Perseus Books Group, 2002)

Lifton, Robert Jay. *Home from the War, Vietnam Veterans Neither Victims nor Executioners* (Simon and Schuster 1973)

Maclear, Michael. *The Ten Thousand Day War, Vietnam: 1945-1975* (St. Martin's Press, 1981)

Moore, Harold G., Galloway, Joseph C. *We Were Soldiers Once-and Young: Ia Trang and the Battle That Changed the War in Vietnam.* (Random House, 1992)

Nolan, Keith William. *Battle for Hue, Tet 1968* (Presidio Press 1983)

Sheehan, Neil. *A Bright Shining Lie: John Paul Vann and America in Vietnam.* (Vintage Books, 1988)

INDEX

A

Adams, Creighton 214
Afghanistan 172
Aliberti, Rosa 155
Allies 163, 197, 210
Ambassador Su 146
American Declaration of Independence 157
American Embassy in Saigon 94
Americanization 205
American Legion 171
American Society of Newspaper Editors 179
AMF (American Machine and Foundry) 122
amphibious tractors. *See* amtracs
amtracs 57
An Loc 149
Anti-War Movement 27
Ap Cha Do 88, 91, 92
Army Chief of Staff 63, 214
Army of the Republic of Viet Nam 62, 63, 64, 79, 93, 94, 96, 108, 109, 110, 111, 149, 205, 206, 211
ARVN. *See* Army of the Republic of Viet Nam
Atlantic Ocean 157
Austria 162

B

B52 bombers 206, 212
Bahamas 141
Balcom, Abner 22
Balcom, Francis 22
Balcom, Horace 22
Bangalore torpedoes 91
Bay of Pigs 190, 207

Belgium 162
Berkley 206
Bict Dong Quan 108
Bien Hoa Air Base 37
Big Red One 88
Bishop Kearney High School 188
Black North 100, 101. *See also* New York; Towns; Hamlin
Bowen, Burton 85
Bowen, Fred 117
Bowen, Howard L. xi, 59, 83, 84, 91, 92
Bowen, Mary Dunn 85
Bowen, Pete 117
Bowen, Ray 117
Bowen-Roe, Debbie 87
Bowen, Sr, Jess 85
bowling pins 122
Boy Scouts 15, 52, 58, 59, 172
Brant, Rudy 117
Britain 33, 162, 163. *See also* England
British Expeditionary Force 162
British Royal Navy 162
Broekhuizen, Robert 133, 175, 220
Brown University 24
Brunswick Bowling 122
Bryant, Reuben 24
Buchs, Chris 56
Buddhism 62, 63, 96
Buelte, Cletus 59
Bullock, Dayton C. 106
Bullock, Gary E. xi, 59, 99, 100, 111
Bullock, Jay 100, 104
Bundy, McGeorge 209
Burma 28
Bushnell, Harley N. 24

C

Cady, Darryl 53, 175, 217
California 69, 204, 206
  San Francisco 201
Calley, William 114, 115
Cambodia xi, 14, 27, 30, 129, 130, 148, 205, 212, 219, 222
campanilismo 159
Camp Hanson 68
Camp Pendleton 68, 69
Canada 156
Captain Webb 56
Cartier 169
Case, Bryan 49, 173, 217
Case, David 49, 50, 59, 173
Case, Edwin 50, 53
Case, Paul 50
Case, Pauline 52
Case, Peter 50
Case, Susan 50, 51
Castro, Fidel 207
Catholicism 30, 62, 64, 93, 115, 124
Central America 190
Century Magazine 159
Cham 29
Champa. *See* Vietnam; South Vietnam
Chanel 169
Charlie Company 113, 114
Chennault, Anna 204
Chiang Kai-shek 195
China 27, 29, 31, 32, 33, 34, 54, 63, 106, 131, 179, 189, 192, 193, 195, 197, 204, 210, 212
  Hong Kong 195
Chris Taylor (character). *See* Sheen, Charlie
Churchill, Winston 162
Church of St. Francis Xavier 64
CIA 64
Citadel 213

Civil Rights Movement 27
Civil War. *See* Wars; Civil
Claymore mines 90, 109
Clifford, Clark 177
Clinton, DeWitt 18, 19
Cochran, Robert 57
Cold War. *See* Wars; Cold
Committee of the Peasants' International Congress 195
Communist 13, 32, 130, 150, 169, 172, 178, 180, 190, 195, 197, 198, 199, 201, 210, 216
Communist Politburo 199
Conein, Lucien 64
Confucius 29
Congress 82, 190, 194, 195, 201
Connecticut 18, 23, 24
Durham
23
cooper 121
Crandall, Jacob 172
Crandall, John 172
Crimea 195
Cronkite, Walter 93, 97, 218
Cuba 190, 208
Cuban Missile Crisis 208
Cub Scouts 52
Cunard Company 156

D

Daggett, Artemas 25
Dai Vet. *See* Vietnam; North Vietnam
Da Nang 33, 182
D'Andrea, Ryan 171
Danny Boy 77
Davis, John P. xi, 35
Day, Austin 24
De Castries, Christian Marie Ferdinand de la Croix 46

Defillips, Marsha 172, 185, 187
DeFrank, Todd 153
Democratic Republic of Vietnam 32, 146, 179, 198, 210
Democrats 204
Denmark 163
Den Mother. *See* Boy Scouts
Dennis, Janet 85, 87, 92, 218
Depuy, William E. 88
Dien Bien Phu xi, 13, 34, 43, 44, 46, 94, 178, 190, 198, 203, 211
Dinh Bo Linh 29
Disciples United Methodist Church 107. *See also* First Methodist Episcopal Church of Holley
Dolan, Radie 85
Domino Theory 179, 201, 224
Dong Nai. *See* Rivers; Dong Nai
Donitz, Karl 163
Doors (band) 154
  Light My Fire 154
Douglass, Frederick 21
Doumer, Paul 31
DRV 146, 148, 149, 181
Duffey-Mott 165
Dunn, Mike 63
dyspepsia 24

E

Eastertide Offensive 148, 221. *See also* Operation Eastertide
Eastman Kodak 72
Eastman School of Music 187
Eberhardt, Chuck 171
Eisenhower, Dwight D.. *See* United States Presidents; Eisenhower, Dwight D.
Elba Mucklands 117
Ellicot, Joseph 19
Ellis Island 157, 158
Emperor Bao Dai 196, 203

England. *See* Britain
Bristol 156
Dover 162
Liverpool 156
English Channel 162
Erie Canal 18, 19, 20, 21, 36
Erie Canal Commission 19
Europe 121, 141, 161, 163, 195
Evolution of the War. *See* Pentagon Papers

F

famiglia 156, 164
First Methodist Church of Holley 104, 105
First Methodist Episcopal Church of Holley 105, 106
First Presbyterian Church 53
Fischer, George W. xi, 59, 71, 92, 133, 134, 135, 136, 137, 139, 140, 141, 142, 143, 144, 171
Florida 89
Panama City
89
Folia 156. *See also* Principe di Piemonte; *See also* Principello
Ford, Gerald. *See* United States Presidents; Ford, Gerald
Ford, Henry, II 207
Ford Motor Company 207
France 13, 30, 31, 32, 34, 43, 44, 45, 46, 47, 61, 94, 146, 162, 178, 190, 194, 195, 196, 197, 198, 199, 203, 210, 211
Dunkirk (port) 162
Paris 31, 148, 149, 150, 191, 192, 193, 195, 199, 200, 204, 222
Reims 163
Fredonia State Teachers College 187
French Communist Party 195
French East India Company 30
French Indochina 30, 199
French Socialist Party 195
French Union 43, 197
Frisbie, Hiram 20, 24, 105

Full Metal Jacket (movie) 96
Fulton Fish Market 160

G

Gaylord, James 117
General Giap. *See* Vo Nguyen Giap
General Motors 195
Geneva Accords 13, 177, 198. *See also* Pentagon Papers
Geneva agreement 191
Geneva Conventions 178
Geneva Settlement 178, 199
Germany 32, 33, 36, 125, 162, 163, 191
  Berlin 163
Gibson, Irene M. 105
Goldwater, Barry 201
Good, Duane 69, 217
Graham, Billy 111
Great Hunger 206
grenades 90, 91, 167
guerilla warfare 43, 47, 210
Gulf of Thailand 27
Gulf of Tonkin 14, 27, 79, 80, 82, 201, 208, 213
Gulf of Tonkin Resolution 14, 82, 201

H

Haig, Al 192
Haiphong 148
Hamlin, Aerovester 19
Han Dynasty 29
Hanoi 29, 31, 79, 93, 146, 147, 148, 149, 150, 169, 181, 192, 193, 194, 196, 197, 199, 200, 201, 204, 205, 206, 210, 212, 214, 217, 222
Harrison, William Henry. *See* United States Presidents; Harrison, William Henry
Harvard 206
Hawaii 113, 141, 201
  Honolulu 82

Henderson, John Jr 121
hepatitis 39, 40, 41, 217
Herrick, John J. 80, 81, 82, 208
Hersh, Seymour 115
Hillside Cemetery 59, 60, 77, 172, 224
Hillside Cemetery Memorial 172
Hinds, Darius 25
Hinds, Franklin 25
Hinds, Jacob 25
Hinds, Joel 25
Hitler, Adolph 161, 163
Hoang Tru 194
Ho Chi Minh 13, 32, 33, 34, 43, 47, 61, 79, 97, 179, 190, 191, 194, 196, 197, 198, 199, 202, 203, 205, 210, 211, 222
Ho Chí Minh City 32. *See also* Saigon
Holley Baptist Church 23
Holley Cemetery 60
Holley High 36, 58, 134, 137, 138, 187
Holley High School Marching Band 138, 183
Holley, Myron 18, 20, 21, 22, 224
Holley Volunteer Fire Department 36
Holy Cross Cemetery 59
Hong Kong. *See* China; Hong Kong
hooper 121
House of Representatives 200
House, Sally 18
Hue 96, 206, 225
Humphrey, Hubert 202, 204
Huy Duc 170

I

Idaho 160
Independence Palace 151
India Company 30, 56, 57
Indiana
  Indianapolis

52
Indochina 30, 31, 32, 33, 43, 47, 79, 130, 179, 190, 191, 194, 195, 196, 197, 199, 201, 210
Indo-Chinese Communist Party 195, 198
Indonesia 28
Ireland 206
Island of Tears 158. *See also* Ellis Island
Italy 145, 155, 156, 159, 160, 162, 195
  Naples 155
  Palermo 155
  Sciacca 155
  Sicily 155, 164

J

James, Kirk J. 92
Japan 32, 33, 106, 163
  Okinawa 69
Java 28
Jenkins, Mike 55
Jodl, Alfred 163
Johnson, David R. 167
Johnson, Elisha 22
Johnson, Linda 75, 78, 173
Johnson, Lyndon B.. *See* United States Presidents; Johnson, Lyndon B.
Joy, Raymond 68
Justification of the War. *See* Pentagon Papers

K

Keitel, William 163
Kennedy, John F.. *See* United States Presidents; Kennedy, John F.
Kennedy, Robert 204, 209
Kenney, John 171
Kent State University 14, 131, 132, 219
Khe Sanh 93, 94, 211, 212
Khmer Rouge 130, 131, 212
Khrushchev, Nikita 189, 190, 208

Kissinger Associates 194
Kissinger, Henry 147, 149, 191, 194, 198
Klafehn, Karl 102, 103, 163
Klafehn, Minnie 102
Koppel, Ted 199
Korea 106, 189, 213
Kubrick, Stanley 96
Ky Vinh 108

L

Lancaster Speedway 92, 134, 136
Laos 27, 30, 44, 148, 210
Le Duc Tho 147, 148, 149, 150, 191, 192, 193, 198, 199, 200, 204, 222
Le Dynasty 30
Lenin, Vladimir 195
leptospirosis 41, 217
Lerlan, Melissa 172
Lewis, Stephen 19
Libertas 157
Lloyd Sabaudo 156
Lodge, Henry Cabot 63
Long Binh 36, 37, 38, 42
Lord's Prayer 77
Louie 156, 157, 160
Lovett, Robert 207

M

MACV 79, 108, 109, 110, 111, 149, 181, 182, 213, 214, 218
MACV-SOG. *See* Military Assistance Command, Vietnam-Studies and Observation Group
Macy's Thanksgiving Day Parade 138, 139
Maine 107
Mai Van Bo 147
malaria 102, 155, 196
Malayo-Polynesian People 28
Malaysia 28

Mandracchia, Leslie 160, 220
Mandracchia, Louie 155, 164
Mandracchia, Norah 161
Mandracchia, Onofrio Roberto 160
Mandracchia, Paul S. xi, 153, 154, 166, 167
Mandracchia, Rosalie 155, 156, 160
Mandracchia, Sara 172
Manifesto of the National Liberation Front 180
Mansfield, Alanson 23
Mao Zedong 211
Maples, Robert 115
Marine Hymn 78
Martin, Anne 35, 38, 175
Mary Jane Candies 107
Massachusetts 22, 24
  Cities
    Pelham 22
  Counties
    Worcester 24
  Towns
    Templeton 24
McNamara, Robert 82, 177, 206
Mekong Delta. *See* Rivers; Mekong
Memorial Day 171, 172, 173
Men in Black 196
meningitis 41
Merrill, Arch 17
Merrill-Grinnell Funeral Home 142
Methodist Youth Fellowship 71
Mexico 141
Michigan 141
Military Assistance Command, Vietnam-Studies and Observation Group 79, 108, 109, 110, 111, 149, 181, 182, 213, 214, 218
Military Awards
  Bronze Star 15, 110, 111
  Congressional Medal of Honor 91

Gallantry Cross with Palm 167
Medal of Honor 56, 91
Purple Heart 15
Silver Star 15, 73, 75, 200
Vietnamese Cross for Gallantry 15, 167
mineral lick. *See* salt-lick
Minnesota 100
Plainview
100
Montgomery, Bernard 163
Moreland, William C. 79
Morrison, Jim 154
Morrow, Charles 123, 124
Moscow. *See* Russia; Moscow
Mount Etna 155, 165
Mt. Albion Cemetery 124
muck 117, 118, 120
My Lai xi, 113, 114, 115, 215, 219
My Lai Massacre xi, 113, 215, 219

N

Napoleonic Codes of 1804 31
National Archives 177
National Guard 14, 131, 132
National Legislative Conference 147
National Liberation Front 94, 95, 97, 147, 148, 150, 180, 181, 191, 192, 201. *See also* NLF
National Security Advisor 191, 209
Navarre, Henri 43, 44, 45, 211
Nelson, Patricia (Fischer) 142, 171
Netherlands 163
Rotterdam 156
New England 107
New Hampshire 107, 204
New Jersey 109, 159
New Look program 189

Newspapers
  Cleveland Plain Dealer 115
  Democrat & Chronicle 49, 76, 123, 188
  Newsweek 115
  Rochester Freeman 21
  Times 115
New York 14, 18, 22, 23, 24, 25, 49, 52, 60, 69, 75, 91, 101, 105, 111, 134, 138, 139, 155, 156, 157, 159, 164, 183, 187, 195, 199, 217, 218, 221, 222, 224, 225
  Cities
    Albany 18
    Batavia 20, 165
    Buffalo 18, 20
    Canandaigua 18, 20
    Elmira 60
    New York 49, 91, 138, 139
      Bronx 159
      Brooklyn 159, 160, 164, 195
      Manhattan 159
    Niagara Falls 187
    Rochester v, 14, 20, 21, 22, 35, 59, 72, 133, 164, 171, 173
    Syracuse 111, 184, 218
  Counties
    Livingston 24
    Oneid 23
    Ontario 22
    Orleans 22, 24, 59, 117, 119, 187, 216, 218, 224
    Otsego 22
  Towns
    Albion 24, 53, 124, 154
    Caledonia 24
    Clarendon 22, 23, 85, 172, 184
    Greece 134
    Hamlin 19, 20, 101
    Kendall 154, 184
    Kuckville Hamlet 101

LeRoy 25
Murray 22, 23, 24, 25
Villages
Brockport 53, 121, 184
Granville 24
Holley ii, iii, xi, 14, 15, 17, 18, 19, 20, 21, 22, 23, 24, 26, 35, 36, 39, 49, 52, 53, 58, 59, 60, 68, 70, 71, 75, 77, 92, 101, 104, 105, 106, 107, 111, 117, 121, 134, 137, 138, 139, 140, 141, 142, 144, 154, 164, 165, 167, 170, 171, 172, 173, 175, 183, 184, 185, 187, 188, 216, 218, 224
Saltport 19, 22. *See also* New York; Villages; Holley
New York State Fair 183
Ngo Dinh Diem xi, 13, 61, 62, 63, 64, 65, 79, 96, 179, 180, 181, 203, 217
Ngo Dinh Nhu 13, 61, 64
Ngo Quyen 29
Nguyen Ai Quoc. *See* Ho Chi Minh
Nguyen Sinh Cung. *See* Ho Chi Minh
Nguyen Tat Thanh. *See* Ho Chi Minh
Nguyen Van Thieu 148, 149, 150, 191, 192, 193, 199, 204
Nightline (television) 199
Nixon, Richard M.. *See* United States Presidents; Nixon, Richard M.
NLF 95, 97, 148, 150, 180, 181, 191, 192, 201. *See also* National Liberation Front
Nobel Prize 193
Norway 145, 146
NVA 68, 73, 74, 88, 89, 90, 91, 94, 96, 97, 109, 110, 111, 113, 129, 130, 151, 182, 192, 205, 206, 209, 211, 212, 213

O

Oak Orchard Bowling Alley 53, 154
Office of Statistical Control 206
Ohio 14, 131, 145, 219
Ohio National Guard 14
Okinawa. *See* Japan; Okinawa
Oklahoma (theatre) 71
O'Malley, Robert 56
Operation Attleboro 88
Operation Dynamo 162

Operation Eastertide 205, 212. *See also* Eastertide offensive
Operation Linebacker 149, 150
Operation Linebacker II 150
Operation Menu 205
Operation Piranha 57
Operation Rolling Thunder 182, 202, 209
Operation Starlite 54, 55
opium 31
OSS. *See* US Office of Strategic Services

P

Paleolithic Era 28
Paris Peace Accord 200
Peatross, Oscar F. 57
Pennsylvania 92, 145
Pentagon 54, 58, 76, 147, 172, 175, 177, 182, 209, 220, 225
Pentagon Papers 147, 177, 182, 209, 220, 225
People's Republic of North Vietnam. *See* North Vietnam
pettifogging 24
Pham Quyunh 28
Philippines 64
Phnom Penh 130, 131
Phuoc Vinh 88, 89
Pierce, Aretas 23
Pierpont, William 24
Pinguet, Jean 56
Pinkville. *See* Quan Ngai Province
Platoon (movie) 113
Pol Pot 130
Pop Louie's Fish Market 160
Popular Republic of Vietnam 43
potash 24
Potsdam Conference 33
President Diem. *See* Ngo Dinh Diem
President Thieu. *See* Nguyen Van Thieu
Preston, Loren 59, 175, 217

Price, Hubbard 22
Prime Minister 61, 162, 203
Prince Sihanouk 130, 205
Principe de Piemonte 155
Principello 156. *See also* Principe di Piemonte
Procol Harum (band) 154
  A Whiter Shade of Pale 154
Purple Hearts 15

Q

Quang Ngai Province 114
Quang Tin Province 67, 73
Quealy, Mike 91

R

Ramsey, Bertram 162
Ramsey, Fred 111, 219
Reader's Digest 107
Re d'Italia 156
Red Menace 189, 190, 201
Red River Delta. *See* Rivers; Red River
Reed, John 19
Regina d'Italia 156
Report of the Office of the Secretary of Defense Vietnam Task Force. *See* Pentagon Papers
Republican Party 204
Revolutionary Youth League 32
Rhode Island 24
Rhodes, James 131
Rice, William 19
Ridenhour, Ron 114
Rivers
  Dong Nai 36
  Genesee 20
  Mekong 28
  Red River 28

Ron 81
Seneca 18, 20
Robinson, Chauncey 23
Robinson, Jane Bowen 88
Rochester Freeman. *See* Newspapers
Rochester Institute of Technology 171
Rochester Red Wings 72
Rochester Taylor Instrument Company 59
Roman Catholic Church 62
Roosevelt, Theodore. *See* United States Presidents; Roosevelt, Theodore
Root, Sharon (Bullock) 108, 111
Rumania 145
Russia 79, 179, 189, 190, 192, 193, 195, 207, 208. *See also* Soviet Union
Moscow 195

S

Saigon 30, 31, 32, 33, 36, 37, 63, 93, 94, 95, 97, 145, 151, 169, 178, 179, 180, 192, 193, 194, 197, 198, 212
salt-lick 19
Sandy Creek Cemetery 59, 142
Scout Leader. *See* Boy Scouts
Secretary of Defense 82, 177, 206, 207
Secretary of State 207
Seneca River. *See* Rivers
Settlement of the Conflict. *See* Pentagon Papers
Seymour, James 20
Shahin, Ray 137, 183, 185, 187, 188
Sheen, Charlie 113
Shepard's Mill 121
Silent Night 77
Sir J. Laing & Sons, Ltd 156
Sisson, Donald 72, 217
Sisson, George 59
Sisson, Jim 73
Sisson, Ronald P. 59, 67, 73, 74, 75, 77
Smiling Through 77

Smith, Charles "C.D." 68, 69
Smith, Isaac 25
Smith, Sally 25
Social Security Act 161
Sound of Music (theatre) 187
South Carolina 213
South China Sea 27, 54
South Pacific 200
South Vietnam. *See* Vietnam
Soviet Union 13, 130, 131. *See also* Russia
Spencer Speedway 134, 135, 137
spy satellites 207
Stalin, Josef 163, 189
States, David P. ix
Statue of Liberty 157
Stedman, Janice 72, 175, 217
Stockdale, James 82
Stone, Oliver 113
Strategic Hamlet Program 181
Stymus, Duane 117, 119, 219
Stymus, Ethel 117
Stymus, Gary L. 59, 117, 122, 124
Stymus, Helen 122, 127
Stymus, Henry 117
Sweden 145, 146, 195

T

Taps 78
Team 99 108, 110, 111
Tet Offensive xi, 93, 95, 97, 113, 146, 182, 202, 204, 211, 212, 214, 218
Texas 68, 200
Thailand 27, 28, 195
Thieu. *See* Nguyen Van Thieu
Tho. *See* Le Duc Tho
Thomas, Arad 22
Tonawanda Swamp 117

Tonucci, Dick 56
Tran Trong Kim 196
Truman, Harry S.. *See* United States Presidents; Truman, Harry S.
tuberculosis 155, 195
Tucker, Spencer 28
Turkey 208
Tuscarora vii

U

Underground Railroad 21
Union Army 22
United States 13, 14, 27, 36, 37, 43, 46, 47, 62, 63, 64, 75, 77, 79, 80, 82, 93, 94, 97, 106, 108, 115, 122, 129, 130, 131, 146, 147, 151, 164, 171, 172, 177, 178, 184, 189, 190, 191, 192, 193, 200, 201, 215, 222, 225
United States Army Vietnam 36, 37
United States Constitution 171
United States Military
  Marines 53, 55, 57, 73, 74, 75, 77, 95, 151, 167, 202
  Navy 14, 53, 80, 162, 200
  US Army Air Force 206
United States Presidents
  Eisenhower, Dwight D. 46, 163, 189, 223
  Ford, Gerald 150
  Harrison, William Henry 22
  Johnson, Lyndon B. 14, 37, 79, 80, 81, 82, 130, 147, 200, 202, 206, 208, 213, 214, 218, 222
  Kennedy, John F. 13, 61, 63, 79, 180, 200, 203, 206
  Nixon, Richard M. 14, 38, 115, 129, 130, 131, 148, 149, 150, 179, 191, 192, 193, 199, 201, 202, 203, 204, 205, 206, 212, 214, 221, 222, 224
  Roosevelt, Theodore 159
  Truman, Harry S. 189
  Wilson, Woodrow 195
United States Presidents; Johnson, Lyndon B. 209
University of Hanoi 210
USAAF. *See* United States Military; US Army Air Force
US Involvement in the Franco-Viet Minh War. *See* Pentagon Papers

CPSIA information can be obtained
at www.ICGtesting.com
Printed in the USA
FSOW02n0041261016
26573FS